table of contents

HOW TO BECOME A CHRISTIAN

Book One

ABOUT THE WRITER *John MacArthur, Jr.*

INTRODUCING *The God Who Loves* — 5

Week of **June 6**	God So Loved the World	6
Week of **June 13**	The Goodness of God	19
Week of **June 20**	The Severity of God	31
Week of **June 27**	Asking Hard Questions	44
Week of **July 4**	The Love of God for Humanity	57
Week of **July 11**	Finding Security in the Love of God	70

Book Two

ABOUT THE WRITERS *Josh McDowell & Bob Hostetler* — 82

INTRODUCING *Beyond Belief to Convictions* — 83

Week of **July 18**	A Crisis of Belief	84
Week of **July 25**	From Beliefs to Convictions	96
Week of **August 1**	The Truth about Truth	108
Week of **August 8**	Proofs of Christ's Deity	120
Week of **August 15**	Is the Bible Reliable?	132
Week of **August 22**	The Meaning of God's Word to Our Lives	144
Week of **August 29**	Because He Lives	156

ABOUT THE WRITERS

John MacArthur

masterWork:
Essential Messages from God's Servants

- Designed for developing and maturing believers who desire to go deeper into the spiritual truths of God's Word.

- Ideal for many types of Bible study groups.

- A continuing series from leading Christian authors and their key messages.

- Based on LifeWay's well-known, interactive model for daily Bible study.

- The interspersed interactive personal learning activities **in bold type** are written by the writer identified on the Study Theme unit page.

- Teaching plans follow each lesson to help facilitators guide learners through lessons.

- Published quarterly.

one of today's foremost Bible teachers, is the author of numerous best-selling books that have touched millions of lives. He is pastor-teacher of Grace Community Church in Sun Valley, California, and president of The Master's College and Seminary. He is also president of Grace to You, the ministry that produces the internationally syndicated radio program *Grace to You* and a host of print, audio, and Internet resources—all featuring John's popular, verse-by-verse teaching. He also authored the notes in *The MacArthur Study Bible*, which has been awarded the Gold Medallion and has sold more than 500,000 copies. John and his wife, Patricia, have four grown children and twelve grandchildren.

For more details about John MacArthur and all his Bible-teaching resources, contact Grace to You at 800-55-GRACE or www.gty.org.

AMY SUMMERS wrote the personal learning activities and teaching plans this quarter. Amy is an experienced writer for LifeWay Bible study curriculum, a mother, and a Sunday School leader from Arden, North Carolina. She is a graduate of Baylor University and Southwestern Baptist Theological Seminary.

ABOUT THIS STUDY

Read the Study Theme Introduction on page 5.

Which lesson description most intrigues you?

_____

Why are you particularly interested in exploring that aspect of God's love?

_____

The God Who Loves

Love is the best known but least understood of all God's attributes. Almost everyone who believes in God these days believes that He is a God of love. I have even met agnostics who are quite certain that *if* God exists, He must be benevolent, compassionate, and loving.

All those things *are* infinitely true about God, of course, but not the way most people think. Because of the influence of modern liberal theology, many suppose that God's love and goodness ultimately nullify His righteousness, justice, and holy wrath. They envision God as a benign heavenly grandfather—tolerant, affable, lenient, permissive, devoid of any real displeasure over sin, who without consideration of His holiness will benignly pass over sin and accept people as they are.

In our pursuit of understanding the love of God and the God who loves, we must be willing to shed a lot of popular, sentimental notions about divine love. Many of our favorite presuppositions about God need to be corrected. God's love and His holiness must be carefully understood in light of His wrath against sin. We must see love from the divine perspective before we can truly grasp the import of God's great love for us. We must open-heartedly embrace all of the biblical data.

My design in these lessons is to try to highlight a broad, balanced cross-section of the biblical data. We'll spend the first lesson looking at God and His love. In the second lesson, we will examine the goodness of God in spite of our sin. In the third lesson, we will focus on the severity of God and His righteous justice. In lesson four, we will deal with how to approach some hard questions related to the God who loves. In the fifth lesson, we'll look at how God's love applies to all humanity and how it applies in a unique and special way to Christians. And in the final lesson, we will analyze the security believers find in the love of God.

John MacArthur

John **MacARTHUR, JR.**

God So Loved the World

What Is Love?

Carefully read 1 John 4:7-21. Which verse about love is especially meaningful to you today? Write it in the space below.

On a cross-country domestic airliner a few years ago, I plugged in the earphones and began to listen to the music program. I was amazed at how much of the music dealt with love. At the time I was preaching through 1 John 4, so the subject of love was very much on my mind. I couldn't help noticing how glib and shallow most of the lyrics were. "She Loves You, Yeah, Yeah, Yeah" is a classic by worldly standards. But few people would argue that its lyrics are truly profound.

I began to realize how easily our culture trivializes love by sentimentalizing it. The love we hear about in popular songs is almost always portrayed as a *feeling*—usually involving unfulfilled desire. Most love songs describe love as a longing, a passion, a craving that is never quite satisfied, a set of expectations that are never met. Unfortunately, that sort of love is devoid of any ultimate meaning. It is actually a tragic reflection of human lostness.

As I thought about it, I realized something else: Most love songs not only reduce love to an emotion, but they also make it an involuntary one. People "fall" in love. They get swept off their feet by love. They can't help themselves. They go crazy for love. One song laments, "I'm hooked on a feeling," while another confesses, "I think I'm going out of my head."

It may seem a nice romantic sentiment to characterize love as uncontrollable passion, but those who think carefully about it will realize that such "love" is both selfish and irrational. It is far from the biblical concept of love. Love, according to Scripture, is not a helpless sensation of desire. Rather, it is a purposeful act of self-giving. The one who

Week of JUNE 6

genuinely loves is deliberately devoted to the one loved. True love arises from the will—not from blind emotion. Consider, for example, this description of love from the pen of the apostle Paul:

> Love is patient, love is kind, and is not jealous; love does not brag and is not arrogant, does not act unbecomingly; it does not seek its own, is not provoked, does not take into account a wrong suffered, does not rejoice in unrighteousness, but rejoices with the truth; bears all things, believes all things, hopes all things, endures all things (1 Cor. 13:4-7).

Read 1 Corinthians 13:4-7 again and underline each attribute of love that is difficult for you to display. Why can't this kind of love be an emotion that ebbs and flows involuntarily?

_____

Love is not a mere feeling. All the attributes of love Paul lists involve the mind and volition. In other words, the love he describes is a thoughtful, willing commitment. Also, notice that genuine love "does not seek its own." That means if I truly love, I'm concerned not with having my desires filled, but with seeking the best for whoever is the object of my love.

So the mark of true love is not unbridled desire or wild passion; it is a giving of oneself. Jesus Himself underscored this when He told His disciples, "Greater love has no one than this, that one lay down his life for his friends" (John 15:13). If love is a giving of oneself, then the greatest love is shown by laying down one's very life. And of course, such love was perfectly modeled by Christ.

What type of love do you most often model? Mark your response on the line below.

|—————|—————|—————|—————|

involuntary   **deliberate**
self-centered feeling   **self-giving choice**

7

Love Is at the Heart of God's Character

The apostle John has been called "the apostle of love" because he wrote so much on the subject. He was fascinated by it, overwhelmed with the reality that he was loved by God. He often referred to himself in his gospel as "the disciple whom Jesus loved" (John 21:20; see 13:23; 20:2; 21:7).

Read 1 John 4:8b-9. What overwhelming conclusions about love had John reached by the time he wrote his first epistle? _____

The words of 1 John 4:8-9 are a clear echo of a familiar passage, John 3:16: "For God so loved the world, that He gave His only begotten Son, that whoever believes in Him should not perish, but have eternal life."

Look carefully, first of all, at this simple phrase from 1 John 4:8: "God is love." There are many ways to *misunderstand* John's meaning. In fact, 1 John 4:8 seems a particular favorite of cultists. All kinds of false sects have misapplied this verse to support wildly heretical notions. In what sense then is it true that God is love?

Dr. MacArthur says the expression "God is love" does NOT:

1. _____

2. _____

3. _____

First, the expression "God is love" is not meant to depersonalize God or portray Him as a force, a sensation, a principle, or some sort of cosmic energy. God is a personal Being, with all the attributes of personality—volition, feeling, and intellect. In fact, what the apostle is saying is that God's love is the highest expression of His person. To use this text to attempt to depersonalize God is to do great violence to the clear meaning of Scripture.

Second, this verse by no means identifies God with everything our society labels love. In fact, those who cite this verse to attempt to legitimize illicit forms of "love" are about as far from the apostle's intent as it is possible to get. The love of which John speaks is a pure and holy love, consistent with all God's divine attributes.

Week of JUNE 6

Third, this assertion is not meant to be a definition of God or a summary of His attributes. Divine love in no way minimizes or nullifies God's other attributes—His omniscience, His omnipotence, His omnipresence, His immutability, His lordship, His righteousness, His wrath against sin, or any of His glorious perfections. Deny any one of them and you have denied the God of Scripture.

There is certainly more to God than love. Similar expressions elsewhere in Scripture demonstrate this.

Read the following Scriptures. Draw a line matching each reference to the statement it makes about God.

Psalm 7:11	God is true
Psalm 99:9	God is a consuming fire
John 3:33	God is Spirit
John 4:24	God is righteous
Hebrews 12:29	God is holy

The simple statement "God is love" obviously does not convey everything that can be known about God. We know from Scripture that He is also holy and righteous and true to His Word. God's love does not contradict His holiness; instead, it complements and magnifies it and gives it its deepest meaning. So we cannot isolate this one phrase from the rest of Scripture and attempt to make love represent the sum of what we know about God.

God is love. But having said that, we have not said everything that is true about God. Nevertheless, we dare not minimize the force of this crucial text. By saying "God is love," the apostle is making a very strong statement about the character and the essence of God. It is God's very nature to love—love permeates who He is.

Clearly the love this text describes is an eternal reality. It flows from the very nature of God and is not a response to anything outside the person of God. The apostle does not say, "God is loving," as if he were speaking of one of many divine attributes, but "God is love"—as if to say that love pervades and influences all His attributes.

For example, we know that God is holy, "undefiled, separated from sinners and exalted above the heavens" (Heb. 7:26). As a holy being, He would be perfectly righteous to view all sinners with the utmost

If you desire to dig deeper…
Read the following Scriptures and make a list of "God is" statements.

- 2 Chronicles 30:9
- Job 36:5
- Psalm 54:4; 62:8; 116:5
- Daniel 5:21; 9:9
- 1 Corinthians 10:13
- 2 Thessalonians 1:6
- 1 John 1:5

contempt. But His is a loving holiness that reaches out to sinners with salvation for them—the antithesis of aloofness or indifference.

Love surely tempers even God's judgments. What a wonder it is that He who is a consuming fire, He who is unapproachable light, is also the personification of love! He postpones His judgments against sin while pleading with sinners to repent. He freely offers mercy to all who will repent. He shows longsuffering and goodness even to many who steel their hearts against Him. Divine love not only keeps divine wrath in check while God appeals to the sinner—but it also proves that God is just when He finally condemns.

And even when He condemns, "God is love." Our God therefore shows Himself to be not only glorious but also good; not only spotlessly holy but also wondrously compassionate; not only righteous but also a God of matchless love. And that love emanates from His very essence.

Complete this prayer.

God, I thank You that You are love because _____

_____

"Only true Christians are capable of genuine love."
—John MacArthur

Love Is From God

From the truth that God is love, the apostle draws this corollary: "Love is from God" (1 John 4:7). God is the source of all true love.

Read 1 John 4:7-8. What is the best evidence that a person truly knows God? (Place a check mark.)
- ❏ **The ability to quote numerous Scripture passages**
- ❏ **A special glow in the eyes**
- ❏ **Complete moral purity**
- ❏ **A demonstrated love for others**

Week of JUNE 6

Love is the proof of a regenerate heart. Only true Christians are capable of genuine love. Clearly, however, the kind of love the apostle is speaking of is a higher, purer form of love than we commonly know from human experience. The love of which he speaks does not flow naturally from the human heart. It is not a carnal love, a romantic love, or even a familial love. It is a supernatural love that is peculiar to those who know God. It is *godly* love.

In fact, the apostle employed a Greek word for "love" that was highly unusual in first-century culture. The word was *agape*, not a common word until the New Testament made it so. When a typical first-century pagan thought of love, *agape* was not the word that would have come to mind. In fact, there were two other common Greek words for love: *phileo*, to describe brotherly love, and *eros*, to describe everything from romantic love to sexual passion.

Phileo is occasionally used in the New Testament as a synonym for *agape*, but generally the word *agape* is used as a more refined and elevated term. In the sense that John uses it here, *agape* is unique to God. He is the sole source of it.

Love for one's family, romantic love, and the love of good friends all fall into the category of what Scripture calls "natural affection" (Rom. 1:31; 2 Tim. 3:3, KJV). Even these expressions of "natural affection," or human love, can be marvelously rich. They fill life with color and joy. They are, however, merely pale reflections of the image of God in His creatures. His love is *perfect* love. It is that pure, holy, godly love that can be known only by those who are born of Him. It is the same unfathomable love that moved God to send "His only begotten Son into the world so that we might live through Him" (1 John 4:9).

Think of persons who show you love—perhaps a spouse, child, or grandchild. How do those human expressions of love give you joy?

Read 1 Corinthians 13:12. How do your earthly loves, with all their joys and delights, compare with the full expression of godly love?

Donald W. Burdick gives three characteristics of this godly sort of love: *It is spontaneous.* There was nothing of value in the persons loved that called forth such sacrificial love. God of His own free will set His love on us in spite of our enmity and sin. *[Agape]* is love that is initiated by the lover because he wills to love, not because of the value or lovableness of the person loved. *It is self-giving. [Agape]* is not interested in what it can gain, but in what it can give. It is not bent on satisfying the lover, but on helping the one loved whatever the cost. *It is active. [Agape]* is not mere sentiment cherished in the heart. Nor is it mere words however eloquent. It does involve feeling and may express itself in words, but it is primarily an attitude toward another that moves the will to act in helping to meet the need of the one loved.[1]

All true believers have this love; and all who have it are true believers. This kind of love cannot be conjured up by the human will. It is wrought in the hearts of believers by God Himself: "We love, because He first loved us" (1 John 4:19). Love for God and love for fellow believers is an inevitable result of the new birth, by which we "become partakers of the divine nature" (2 Pet. 1:4). Just as it is God's nature to love, love is characteristic of His true children: "The love of God has been poured out within our hearts through the Holy Spirit who was given to us" (Rom. 5:5).

Godly love, therefore, is one of the most important tests of the reality of one's faith.

Drawing on the truths from 1 John 4:19; 2 Peter 1:4; and Romans 5:5, complete the sentence below.

I can love others with godly love because _____

_____

_____

Week of JUNE 6

day Four

The One Who Doesn't Love

In John's first epistle, he is writing in part to destroy the *false assurance* of those who may profess faith in Christ without really knowing Him.

Read the following verses and state what John pointed to as evidence that a person doesn't know Christ.
1 John 1:6: _____
1 John 2:4: _____
1 John 2:9: _____

Read 1 John 4:8. What did John state was the litmus test for the true Christian?

_____

Sadly, most of us have encountered professing Christians whose hearts seem bereft of any genuine love. The apostle John's admonition is a solemn reminder that a mere pretension of faith in Christ is worthless. *Genuine* faith will inevitably be shown by love. After all, real faith works through love (Gal. 5:6).

This sort of God-given love is not easily counterfeited. Look at all that is involved: love for God Himself (1 Cor. 16:22); love for the brethren (1 John 3:14); love of truth and righteousness (Rom. 6:17-18); love for the Word of God (Ps. 1:2); and even love for one's enemies (Matt. 5:44). Such love is contrary to human nature. It is antithetical to our natural selfishness. The very thought of loving those things is odious to the sinful heart.

Later in this same chapter of 1 John, the apostle writes, "God is love, and the one who abides in love abides in God, and God abides in him" (v. 16)—again making the godly kind of love the mark of genuine faith.

Here are ten simple, practical ways of knowing whether we abide in love.

"If anyone does not love the Lord, he is to be accursed" (1 Cor. 16:22).

"We know that we have passed out of death into life, because we love the brethren. He who does not love abides in death" (1 John 3:14)

"But thanks be to God that though you were slaves of sin, you became obedient from the heart to that form of teaching to which you were committed, and having been freed from sin, you became slaves of righteousness" (Rom. 6:17-18).

"But his delight is in the law of the LORD, and in His law he meditates day and night" (Ps. 1:2).

"But I say to you, love your enemies and pray for those who persecute you" (Matt. 5:44).

Set aside time to prayerfully read each Scripture in the checklist below and examine whether you are abiding in love.

- ❏ Have I lost the sense that God is against me? (Rom. 5:1; 8:31)
- ❏ Have I lost the craven fear of God and gained a corresponding increase in godly fear? (1 John 4:18; Heb. 12:28)
- ❏ Do I sense the love of God for me? (1 John 4:16)
- ❏ Do I know my sins are forgiven? (Rom. 4:7-8)
- ❏ Do I have a sense of gratitude to God? (Col. 2:6-7)
- ❏ Do I have an increasing hatred for sin? (Rom. 7:15-16)
- ❏ Do I desire to please God and live a holy life? (John 14:21; 1 John 2:5-6)
- ❏ Do I desire to know God better and draw near to Him? (Phil. 3:10)
- ❏ Do I have a conscious regret that my love for God is less than what it ought to be? (Phil. 1:9-10)
- ❏ Do I delight in hearing about God and the things of God? (Ps. 1:1-2)

The Cross Is the Consummate Proof of Divine Love

Noumenon:
An object reached by intellectual intuition, without the aid of the senses.

We would not be doing justice to 1 John 4:8-9 if we limited our discussion of divine love to abstract terms. The love of God is not merely a subjective noumenon. It is dynamic, active, vibrant, and powerful. God has "manifested" His love, or displayed it in a particular act that can be examined objectively.

In other words, Scripture does not merely say "God is love" and leave it to the individual to interpret subjectively what that means. There is a very important doctrinal context in which the love of God is explained and

Week of JUNE 6

illustrated. To affirm that God is love while denying the doctrine underlying and defining that truth is to render the truth itself meaningless.

But that is precisely what many have done. Theological liberals are very keen to affirm that God is love; yet they often flatly deny the significance of Christ's substitutionary atonement. They suggest that because God is love, Christ did not actually need to die as a substitutionary sacrifice to turn away the divine wrath from sinners. They portray God as easy to mollify, and they characterize the death of Christ as an act of martyrdom or a moral example for believers—denying that it was God's own wrath that needed to be propitiated through a blood sacrifice, and denying that He purposely gave His Son in order to make such an atonement. Thus, they reject the consummate manifestation of God's love, even while attempting to make divine love the centerpiece of their system.

> **Read 1 John 4:10. John explained God's love in terms of: (check one)**
> ❑ **Warm fuzzy feelings**
> ❑ **His response to our love for Him**
> ❑ **His desire to make us happy**
> ❑ **Sacrificial atonement for sin**

First John 4:10 speaks of a sacrifice designed to turn away the wrath of an offended deity. What the apostle is saying is that God gave His Son as an offering for sin, to satisfy His own wrath and justice in the salvation of sinners.

This is the very heart of the gospel. The "good news" is not that God is willing to overlook sin and forgive sinners. That would compromise God's holiness. That would leave justice unfulfilled. That would trample on true righteousness. Furthermore, that would not be love on God's part, but apathy.

The *real* good news is that God Himself, through the sacrifice of His Son, paid the price of sin. He took the initiative ("not that we loved God, but that He loved us"). He was not responding to anything in sinners that made them worthy of His grace. On the contrary, His love was altogether undeserved by sinful humanity. The sinners for whom Christ died were worthy of nothing but His wrath.

> **Read Romans 5:7-8. For whom did Christ die?** _____

John MacArthur, Jr.

In what state were you when Christ died for you?

Because God is righteous, He must punish sin; He cannot simply absolve guilt and leave justice unsatisfied. But the death of Christ totally satisfied God's justice, His righteousness, and His holy hatred of sin.

Take away this doctrine of substitutionary atonement and you have no gospel at all. If the death of Christ was anything less than a guilt offering for sinners, no one could ever be saved.

But in Christ's death on the cross, there is the highest possible expression of divine love. He, who is love, sent His precious Son to die as an atonement for sin. If your sense of fair play is outraged by that—good! It ought to be shocking. It ought to be astonishing. It ought to stagger you. Think it through, and you'll begin to get a picture of the enormity of the price God paid to manifest His love.

At the cross God's love is shown to sinful humanity—fallen creatures who have no rightful claim on His goodness, His mercy, or His love. If you catch a glimpse of this truth, your thoughts of God as a loving Father will take on a whole new depth and richness. "God is love"—and He demonstrated His love for us in that while we were sinners in rebellion against Him, He gave His only Son to die on our behalf—and so that we might live through Him (Rom. 5:8; 1 John 4:9-10). That is the very heart of the gospel, and it holds forth the only hope to those in bondage to their sin: "Believe in the Lord Jesus, and you shall be saved" (Acts 16:31).

Read aloud or sing the words to the hymn below. Continue reading or singing it until you begin to grasp the enormity of God's love for you.

I stand amazed in the presence
Of Jesus the Nazarene,
And wonder how He could love me,
A sinner, condemned, unclean.
How marvelous! how wonderful!
And my song shall ever be;
How marvelous! how wonderful!
Is my Savior's love for me![2]

[1] Donald W. Burdick, *The Letters of John the Apostle* (Chicago: Moody Press, 1985), 351.
[2] Charles H. Gabriel, "I Stand Amazed in the Presence," *The Baptist Hymnal* (Nashville: Convention Press, 1991), No. 547.

Week of JUNE 6

NOTES

To the Leader:

The only truly effective lesson comes from a transformed teacher. Work through each day's lessons as a student, prayerfully determining what God wants to say to you. Then work back through the lesson as a teacher, prayerfully determining what God wants to say to each adult in your class. Choose the teaching steps that will engage and challenge your class members. Remember, the teaching steps don't have to be followed exactly. Allow the suggestions to spark your own thoughts and creativity.

Before the Session

1. Compile a list of secular love song titles or lyrics. You may wish to conduct an internet search of "old love songs."
2. Ask volunteers to be prepared to read Mark 10:45; Colossians 1:19-20; and Revelation 5:9.
3. Provide copies of the *The Baptist Hymnal* (1991 edition).

During the Session

1. Welcome participants. Open with prayer requests and prayer.
2. Ask adults to name secular song titles or phrases that speak of love (you may need to share some from your list to get the discussion rolling). Write responses on one side of the board. Ask, *If these songs were the only references to love we had, how might we define love?* Lead the class to formulate a definition of love based on secular love songs.
3. Request a volunteer read 1 John 4:7-12. Ask the class to define love based on God's Word. Allow volunteers to share which verse about love from 1 John 4 is particularly meaningful to them and why.
4. Direct participants to call out attributes of love stated in 1 Corinthians 13. Write responses on the board next to the love songs. Lead the class to compare the world's perception of love to God's declaration of love. Lead a discussion on how each attribute of godly love requires thought and selfless choices.
5. Ask volunteers to look up and read the Scripture passages listed in the margin in Day 2. Guide the class to compile a list of "God is" statements. Inquire: *Why might some people say these statements contradict the truth that God is love? How do these declarations of God's character actually shed light on God's nature of love?*
6. Ask adults to state what Dr. MacArthur says "God is love" does not mean. Discuss why it is important for believers to know what "God is love" does not mean.
7. Organize the class into three groups. Ask Group 1 to read Isaiah 40:1-5 and identify how God's love, justice, and holiness are

17

NOTES

displayed in that passage. Ask Group 2 to do the same with Isaiah 57:15-21 and Group 3 to do the same with Isaiah 65:1-3, 6-7. Allow groups to share. Ask, *How do these passages demonstrate that God is love even when He condemns?*

8. Request a volunteer read aloud the quotation from the margin in Day 3. Ask learners why they agree or disagree with that statement.
9. Allow volunteers to share how their earthly loves give them joy (second activity in Day 3). Ask how the joy from our earthly loves compares to the full expression of God's love.
10. Ask the class to state the three characteristics of *agape* love as described by Donald Burdick. Lead the class to compare these characteristics of *agape* love to *phileo* or *eros* love. Ask how God displays the three characteristics of *agape* love. Challenge learners to state specific ways they can demonstrate these characteristics of *agape* love in their relationships at home, at work, at church, and in the community.
11. Request volunteers share the sentence they completed in the final activity of Day 3.
12. Inquire, *What actions must we take if we completed the checklist in Day 4 and determined that we are not abiding in love?* Refer learners to the inside cover of *MasterWork* and encourage them to prayerfully determine whether they have ever given their lives to Christ.
13. Ask what object the world often uses to symbolize love. Draw a large heart on the board. Request the pre-enlisted volunteers read their verses. Ask the class to state the heart of the gospel. Write responses inside the heart.
14. Remind participants today's session began with a discussion of songs that inaccurately represent love. Encourage them to conclude the session by stating song titles or phrases that illustrate the true expression of love. You may recommend they look through *The Baptist Hymnal* for ideas, particularly pages 132-157. Promote this as a time of praise as you reflect on the amazing love of God. You may choose to read a chorus of one of the hymns as your closing prayer.

After the Session

1. Read next week's lesson and complete the learning activities.
2. Urge learners who want to know more about giving their lives to Christ and abiding in love to speak with you or to a church staff member.

Week of **JUNE 13**

The Goodness of God

Love and Wrath

In spite of the clarity of Scripture on God's love, millions are kept in spiritual darkness by a notion of God that is completely out of balance. They want a God who is loving but not wrathful. The God of Scripture doesn't fit the bill. They therefore worship a god of their own making. Their thoughts about God constitute sheer idolatry.

For this very reason there is an inherent danger in focusing too intently on any one attribute of God, such as His love. The apostle Paul wrote, "Behold therefore the goodness *and* severity of God" (Rom. 11:22, KJV, emphasis added). It is crucial that we maintain the biblical balance in our thinking. While we study God's love, we must bear in mind that God "is a righteous judge, and a God who has indignation every day" (Ps. 7:11).

We must not stress divine love to the extent that we distort these other equally crucial truths about God. Unfortunately, that is precisely the tragic path our culture as a whole has taken. God's wrath is virtually a taboo subject. Most people would be only too willing to relegate the notion of divine wrath to the scrap heap of outmoded or unsophisticated religious ideas.

> "God's wrath and His love are fixed and steady dispositions. They are not moods or passionate emotions."
> —John MacArthur

> **Read Jeremiah 5:11-13,21-25. What attitudes toward God and His prophets do many people in our society share with the people of Jeremiah's day?**

_____

A clarification needs to be made at this point. When we speak of God's love and God's wrath, we are not talking about anything like human passions. God's wrath and His love are fixed and steady dispositions. They are not moods or passionate emotions. He does not swing wildly from one temperament to the other. To think of God that way is to deny that He is eternally unchanging. He Himself says: "I, the Lord, do not change" (Mal. 3:6). With God "there is no variation, or shifting shadow" (Jas. 1:17). He is "the same yesterday and today, yes and forever" (Heb. 13:8).

Nor do God's wrath and love imply any contradiction in His nature. God's wrath is not inconsistent with His love. Because He so completely loves what is true and right, He must hate all that is false and wrong. Because He so perfectly loves His children, He seeks what blesses and edifies them, and hates all that curses and debases them. Therefore, His wrath against sin is actually an expression of His love for His people. And when He exercises vengeance against the enemies of truth, that also reveals His love.

Read Ezekiel 33:11. How do you see God's love expressed through His wrath against sin?

_____

One classic example of this was Nineveh, a city that was Israel's nemesis for several centuries. There both the goodness and the severity of God were dramatically put on display. In fact, nowhere are God's lovingkindness and His holy wrath seen side by side more vividly than in the history of Nineveh. In this lesson we will examine God's goodness to the city, and in next week's lesson we will see how that goodness finally gave way to an awful outpouring of divine wrath.

day two

Sin City

Nineveh was an ancient city founded by Nimrod. Genesis 10:8-12 records that Nimrod founded the entire Babylonian kingdom, of which Nineveh was a part (see Micah 5:6). Nimrod's Babylon became the source of virtually every false religious system.

Week of JUNE 13

Read Revelation 17:5 and complete the following: Scripture describes Babylon as the mother of

_____.

What do you think that means?

_____

From its very beginning, Nineveh was one of the most important cities of the Babylonian empire, steeped in wickedness and debauchery. Nineveh opposed everything the true God stood for and vice versa.

In the eighth century B.C., Nineveh became the capital of Assyria. The Assyrians were known for their wicked ruthlessness. W. Graham Scroggie wrote: "These people ruled with hideous tyranny and violence from the Caucasus and the Caspian to the Persian Gulf, and from beyond the Tigris to Asia Minor and Egypt. The Assyrian kings literally tormented the world. They flung away the bodies of soldiers like so much clay; they made pyramids of human heads; they sacrificed holocausts of the sons and daughters of their enemies; they burned cities; they filled populous lands with death and devastation; they reddened broad deserts with carnage of warriors; they scattered whole countries with the corpses of their defenders as with chaff; they impaled 'heaps of men' on stakes, and strewed the mountains and choked the rivers with dead bones; they cut off the hands of kings, and nailed them on the walls, and left their bodies to rot with bears and dogs on the entrance gates of cities; they cut down warriors like weeds, or smote them like wild beasts in the forests, and covered pillars with the flayed skins of rival monarchs . . . and these things they did without sentiment or compunction."[1]

Read Zephaniah 2:15 in the margin. What adjectives would you use to describe Assyria's mind-set?

_____

> "This is the carefree city that lived in safety. She said to herself, 'I am, and there is none besides me'" (Zeph. 2:15, NIV).

Nineveh represented the seat of this evil culture. Understandably, the Israelites hated Nineveh and all that the Assyrians represented.

**In your opinion, should Nineveh have been given a chance to repent and experience God's love?   ❏ Yes ❏ No
Why, or why not?** _____

John MacARTHUR, JR.

A Reluctant Prophet and a Great Revival

At the very height of Assyrian power, God commanded a prophet of Israel to go to Nineveh and warn the people there of God's impending judgment. Not surprisingly, the prophet rebelled.

That prophet was Jonah, whose history is familiar to every Sunday school student. Commanded by God to go to Nineveh, Jonah boarded a ship in the Mediterranean—and headed the opposite direction! (Jonah 1:3). "The Lord hurled a great wind on the sea . . . so that the ship was about to break up" (v. 4). The sailors on the ship discovered that Jonah had angered God, and on Jonah's own instructions they threw him overboard (vv. 12-15).

God had prepared a great fish to be at precisely the right spot, and the fish swallowed Jonah (v. 17). After three days and nights in the fish's belly—time spent by the disobedient prophet praying one of the finest prayers of repentance recorded in Scripture—Jonah was miraculously spared (2:1-9): "The Lord commanded the fish, and it vomited Jonah up onto the dry land" (2:10).

Read Jonah 3:1-3 and do the following:

Circle all the adjectives you think describe the tone of voice God used to command Jonah a second time.

Furious   Calm   Exasperated   Patient   Firm

Circle all the adverbs that describe how you think Jonah responded to that command.

Exuberantly   Reluctantly   Terrified

Carefree   Begrudgingly

Week of JUNE 13

Have you ever noticed *why* Jonah attempted to flee Nineveh? It was not because he feared the city's inhabitants. It was not that he was intimidated by the thought of preaching God's Word to pagans. Nothing indicated that Jonah was the least bit timid in the face of the Lord's enemies. In fact, what little we know about him proves he was not a particularly shy man.

Read Jonah 4:2 in the margin and underline what Jonah knew to be true about God.

Why did Jonah's knowledge of God lead him to resist the command to warn Nineveh of God's wrath?

_____

"He prayed to the LORD, 'O LORD, is this not what I said when I was still at home? That is why I was so quick to flee to Tarshish. I knew that you are a gracious and compassionate God, slow to anger and abounding in love, a God who relents from sending calamity'" (Jonah 4:2, NIV).

Because Jonah knew God loves sinners and seeks to save them, Jonah did not want to warn the Gentile Ninevites. He preferred to keep silent and allow God's judgment to take them by surprise. He would have been happiest if God had wiped the Ninevites from the face of the earth without any warning. His worst fear was that the city would repent, and then God would forestall His judgment.

That is, in fact, precisely what happened. Jonah had barely been in Nineveh one day when a remarkable spiritual awakening rocked the place. Jonah's message was short: "Yet forty days and Nineveh will be overthrown" (3:4). At that simple warning, Scripture tells us, "The people of Nineveh believed in God; and they called a fast and put on sackcloth from the greatest to the least of them" (v. 5). This pagan city repented of the evil they had done. The revival went through the entire population (estimated at about 600,000). Even the king "arose from his throne, laid aside his robe from him, covered himself with sackcloth, and sat on the ashes" (v. 6). It was the most extraordinary spiritual revival the world had ever seen. To this day history has never seen another awakening like what happened in Nineveh.

But Jonah was *not* pleased. His worst fear was coming to pass before his eyes. Still, he hoped to see God's judgment carried out. He camped on the east side of the city to see what would happen (4:5). What *did* happen is not as familiar to most people as Jonah's experience with the fish. But it reveals the main point of the Book of Jonah. God was giving Jonah a lesson about the glory of divine compassion.

Read Jonah 4:6-11.

> What do you think? Do you think Jonah's attitude changed and he became a compassionate man who cared about all people? Write your thoughts here.

That is surely one of the strangest finales in all Scripture. We are not told what became of Jonah. We have no idea whether his attitude changed after this, or if he remained the entire forty days, still hoping for the destruction of Nineveh. We get no glimpse of how Jonah responded in his heart to the Lord's tender admonition. We know nothing of his further ministry. History is even silent about the long-term effects of the revival in Nineveh. But the lesson God was teaching Jonah—and all Israel—was very clear. God is loving, merciful, patient, and compassionate toward sinners.

What happened to the prophecy of Nineveh's destruction? "When God saw their deeds, that they turned from their wicked way, then God relented concerning the calamity which He had declared He would bring upon them. And He did not do it" (3:10). Does this imply some changeableness in God? The *King James Version* is even more forceful: "God *repented* of the evil, that he had said that he would do unto them; and he did it not" (emphasis added). Is that not a contradiction of Numbers 23:19: "God is not a man, that He should lie, nor a son of man, that He should repent; has He said, and will He not do it? Or has He spoken, and will He not make it good?"

But this is no contradiction; it is an *anthropopathism*—a figure of speech that assigns human thoughts and emotions to God. Scripture uses anthropopathisms to explain to us truths about God that cannot be expressed in literal human terms.

Jonah 3:10 does not mean that God actually changed His mind. Quite the contrary; it was the Ninevites who changed. The turning away of God's wrath was perfectly consistent with His eternal loving character. Indeed, if He had *not* stayed His hand against Nineveh, *that* would have signaled a change in God.

Read Jeremiah 18:7-8. What overrides God's threatened judgments?

_____

_____

Week of JUNE 13

The prophecy of doom against Nineveh was issued against a people who were haughty, violent, God-hating pagans. No such threat is ever uttered against humble penitents clothed in sackcloth and ashes. The revival utterly changed the people of Nineveh, so God stayed His hand of judgment and forgave them out of His love.

What happened was, of course, God's design from the beginning. Jonah seemed to understand this. He sensed that the prophetic warning was intended by God to turn the hearts of the Ninevites. That was why he fled toward Tarshish at the outset.

Three Things God Appointed

Throughout the Book of Jonah we see God at work in divine providence, sovereignly orchestrating all events in accordance with His eternal purposes. We are told, for example, that God appointed the fish that swallowed Jonah (1:17). Now in the closing chapter of the book, we read three times that God "appointed" certain things to be graphic illustrations to Jonah as God taught the prophet a lesson about divine compassion. God was sovereignly directing everything, not only for the Ninevites' good, but for Jonah's good as well—even though what ensued was not entirely to Jonah's liking.

God gave the pouting prophet a series of object lessons to rebuke his lack of love for the people of Nineveh.

Read Jonah 4:6-8 and complete the following.

God appointed: 1. _____, 2. _____, and 3. ___ _____.

How did Jonah feel about the first item God sent to him? Why?

_____

Jonah probably saw the plant as a token of God's favor to Him. Perhaps he thought he could read the hand of divine providence in this event. After all, a single plant miraculously shooting up in the middle of the desert in just the right place to provide shade for Jonah *must* signify that God was on his side, not on the side of the Ninevites! Jonah might have even thought it meant God was preparing to destroy Nineveh after all. The prophet's mood immediately changed from anger to delight.

But at dawn of the very next day God *appointed a worm,* which attacked the plant so that it withered and died. Worse, God *appointed a hot wind* that sapped all the prophet's strength and suddenly made his circumstances thoroughly uncomfortable.

God was still working all things for Jonah's good, but the prophet did not see it that way. His mood changed again. Now he was angrier than ever. He even begged God to let Him die.

> "Then God said to Jonah, 'Do you have good reason to be angry about the plant?' And he said, 'I have good reason to be angry, even to death' " (Jonah 4:9, NASB).

Check all the reasons you think Jonah was angry.
- ❏ He was embarrassed his threats of judgment against Nineveh wouldn't occur.
- ❏ He wanted to transplant that vine at home.
- ❏ He'd lost a source of personal comfort.
- ❏ He wanted to see Nineveh burn.
- ❏ He wanted God to love only the nation of Israel.

God rebuked the wayward prophet for his failure to understand divine compassion. He reminded Jonah that Nineveh was filled with young children ("more than 120,000 persons who do not know the difference between their right and left hand"). They would all be destroyed if God poured out His wrath on the city. The Lord pointed out that Jonah was so selfish about his own personal comfort that he had more feeling for the plant than for the people of Nineveh.

Notice how Jonah's irrational feelings for the plant ("for which you did not work, and which you did not cause to grow") contrast with God's compassion for His own creation: "Should I not have compassion on Nineveh, the great city?" If God chose to be merciful to the inhabitants of Nineveh, He had every right to display His saving love that way. On the other hand, Jonah—himself a recipient of God's wondrous grace—had *no* right to resent God's compassion for others. He also had no right to be so devoid of compassion toward these people.

Week of JUNE 13

From a human perspective, it is certainly understandable that Jonah, together with virtually all of Israel, would have preferred that God simply destroy Nineveh. But the human perspective is flawed. God is a God of patience, compassion, and grace. Because God was willing to show mercy to a wicked society, Jonah's preaching ushered in one of the most remarkable revivals in the history of mankind—in spite of Jonah himself. And God was glorified in such a display of His great love for sinners.

Does your compassion for others, even the wicked, more closely resemble Jonah or God? Mark your response on the scale below.

|—|—|—|—|—|—|—|—|—|—|

Jonah   **God**

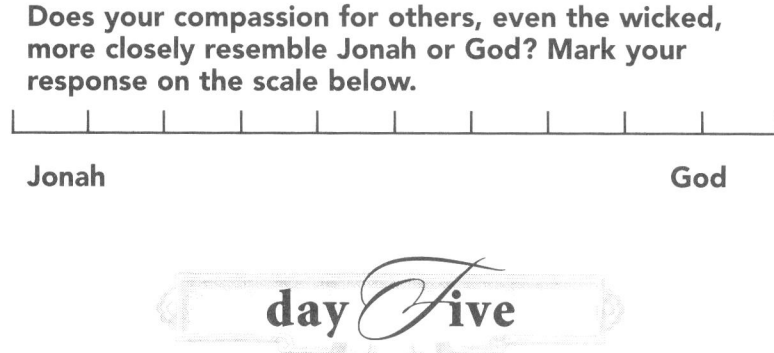

God's Gift of Repentance

God's lovingkindness and tender mercies lavished on such an evil culture give us insight into the very heart of God. It is His nature to love, to show mercy, and to have compassion. But mark this carefully: when God stayed His hand of judgment in Nineveh, He did not merely overlook the sins of that society and allow them to continue blithely in their pursuit of evil. He changed the hearts of the Ninevites. The revival was a miracle wrought by God. As Jonah himself testified, "Salvation is of the Lord" (2:9). God is the One who brought the Ninevites to repentance. He awakened them spiritually so that they mourned for their sins (3:8). They turned from their wicked way (3:10). True repentance from sin is always a gift of God. The Ninevites' repentance was confirmation of the sovereign grace and loving mercy of God.

"True repentance of sin is always a gift of God."
—John MacArthur

On the top of the next page, describe a time you repented of your sin and experienced personal revival. Explain how God's love was confirmed to you in that experience.

The Ninevites turned from their sins, and almost immediately: "The people of Nineveh believed in God; and they called a fast and put on sackcloth from the greatest to the least of them" (3:5). The king shed his kingly garments, put on sackcloth, and proclaimed a fast. It was astonishing that a culture of wicked arrogance could be instantly reduced en masse to the lowest humility in sackcloth and ashes.

What were the long-term effects of this revival? Neither Scripture nor history give us much information. What we know is not encouraging. Sadly, within a generation or so after this revival, Nineveh reverted to her old ways. As we shall see in the following lesson, God finally had to pour out His wrath on the city.

Read Jonah 3:5-9 and record actions and attitudes that demonstrate the Ninevites' response to God.

Read 2 Kings 18:17-35 and note actions and attitudes that describe the Assyrians' response to God just a short time after He spared their city.

What personal warning do you gain from this comparison?

---

[1]W. Graham Scroggie, *The Unfolding Drama of Redemption*, 3 vols. (Grand Rapids: Zondervan Publishing House, 1970 reprint) 1:383.

Week of JUNE 13

Before the Session
1. Read *During the Session*. Choose the teaching steps you will use in your teaching plan.

During the Session
1. Welcome participants. Open with prayer requests and prayer.
2. Guide the class to come up with opposite statements, such as: "If you're inside, you can't be outside." "If you're hot, you can't be cold." After you've had some fun with this, ask: *If God is love, He can't be wrath. Is that true? Why, or why not?* Use the material in Day 1 to discuss why God's love and wrath are not opposite or inconsistent aspects of His character.
3. Ask a volunteer to read 2 Samuel 22:8-16. Ask if people are comfortable with this description of an angry God and why. Request someone read 2 Samuel 22:17-20. Ask how participants feel to read such a tender portrayal of God's love on the heels of such a vivid account of His wrath. Inquire: *Which passage describes the God the world wants to believe in? How can we help people understand God's severity is part of His goodness?* Discuss the final activity in Day 1.
4. Ask participants which description of the Assyrians in Day 2 was particularly disturbing to them and why. Ask: *Do you think the Assyrian Empire should have had a chance to experience God's love or should they have been given over to His wrath? Why?* Ask adults which nations in recent history they thought of as they read the description of the Assyrians. Ask: *Do you think these nations should have a chance to repent and experience God's love or should they face only His wrath? What is our responsibility, if any, to those nations we consider evil?*
5. Ask: *What was Jonah's responsibility toward Nineveh? Did he accept it? Would you? Why, or why not?* Ask learners what they thought of Jonah—what were his weaknesses and his admirable qualities. Comment that it might be difficult to like Jonah partly because he reminds us so much of ourselves. Invite someone to read Jonah 3:1-2. Ask, *How had Jonah experienced God's love and wrath so far?*

NOTES

To the Leader:

"Brothers, if someone is caught in a sin, you who are spiritual should restore him gently. But watch yourself, or you also may be tempted" (Gal. 6:1).

Bible teachers, like Jonah, sometimes have the unpleasant task of confronting a fellow believer about sin. However, unlike Jonah, teachers are not to approach the wayward believer with glee or anger, hoping to see that member experience great punishment. If God commands you to confront a class member about sin in the member's life, do so with great humility, love, and soul-searching, and only after much prayer.

NOTES

6. Request someone read Jonah 3:3-10. Lead a discussion with questions, such as: *How do you think Jonah felt to receive love and a second chance from God? How do you think he felt delivering a message of God's wrath against Nineveh? How did the Ninevites respond? How did God respond?*
7. Request the class silently read Jonah 4:1-4 and state how Jonah responded to the events in Nineveh. Ask why Jonah was so angry. Challenge the class to give examples of how believers today might desire to see the wicked experience only God's wrath and become angry when sinners experience God's love.
8. Direct adults to recall the three entities from nature God used to communicate with Jonah and the lessons He sought to teach Jonah through each one. Ask: *Do you think Jonah learned his lesson? Why, or why not?*
9. Read Jonah 4:11. Ask adults if the conclusion of the Book of Jonah leaves them with the same feeling as a movie with a cliffhanger ending, and why. Ask: *Why do you think God left the story that way? Why didn't God give us some closure?* Challenge the class to work together to create several alternate endings to chapter 4 that tell what happened in Jonah's life after his experience at Nineveh.
10. Ask adults how they discern God's love and wrath in their daily lives. Ask, *What should happen to us as a result of our close-up observation of God's love and wrath?*
11. Review your study of Jonah by asking: *What did you learn about God through this study of Jonah? What did you learn about God's people? How does the difference between God and people help you appreciate God's love even more?*
12. Introduce a time of silent prayer, urging learners to repent of their sins. Encourage volunteers to voice prayers of gratitude for God's love. Close in prayer that each adult present would be a willing messenger of God's goodness and severity.

After the Session

1. Read next week's lesson and complete the learning activities.
2. Encourage participants to not let the summer schedule get them out of the habit of weekly Bible study and worship attendance.
3. Let absentees know they were missed.

Week of JUNE 20

The Severity of God

day One

Nahum: God As Judge

More than a hundred years passed from the time of Jonah until Nahum prophesied the final doom of Nineveh.

Nahum, like Jonah before him, was called specifically to prophesy against that city. The brief Old Testament book that bears his name is his only known prophecy.

Read Nahum 1:2 in the margin. Judging from this verse, what do you think will be the subject of Nahum's prophecy to Nineveh? _____

> "A jealous and avenging God is the LORD; The LORD is avenging and wrathful. The LORD takes vengeance on His adversaries, and He reserves wrath for His enemies" (Nah. 1:2, NASB).

Jonah's message had brought a loving warning to the city. Nahum's message would be a pronouncement of doom. God was about to glorify Himself again, but now He would do it by displaying His wrath against Nineveh.

Shortly after Jonah's experience in Nineveh, the Assyrians—led by Sennacherib [suh-NAK-uh-rib], whose palace was in Nineveh—stepped up their barbarous treatment of the Israelites. Assyrian rulers of this era were ruthless men who boasted of their own brutalities. They liked to torture their victims with slow, cruel means of death, and they were known for building monuments to their conquests out of mutilated human remains. Sennacherib was the worst of the lot.

Assyria was responsible for dragging the ten northern tribes of Israel off into captivity from which they never returned. The Assyrians under Sennacherib also came in military force against the southern kingdom during Hezekiah's reign.

Imagine a Hebrew child asking, "Grandpa, why are the Assyrians our enemies?"

How would a grandfather from the Northern Kingdom of Israel answer? See 2 Kings 15:19-20 and 2 Kings 18:9-11. _____

How would a grandfather from the Southern Kingdom of Judah answer? See 2 Kings 18:13-16.

_____

Through Nahum, God was in effect saying He would no longer tolerate the sins of such a nation or the persecution of His people. And since Nineveh was the capital city of Assyria, it was against the Ninevites that God pronounced His judgment.

Under Jonah's ministry—and despite Jonah's unsympathetic attitude—God displayed His love and compassion for the citizens of Nineveh. Now He would pour out His wrath. Either way, He received glory.

Nahum's prophecy gives us lucid insight into the character of God. Lest we behold His mercy and forget His severity, here is a reminder that ultimately a holy God must wreak vengeance against sin. God is a righteous Judge. For Him to fail to carry out judgment would be inconsistent with His glory, untrue to His Word, and a contradiction of who He is. In other words, the basis for His judgment is His own righteous character. His judgment is as essential to His glory as His love.

In the most candid, vivid terms, Nahum sets forth the majestic character of God as Judge. Nahum's prophecy is noteworthy for its careful balance. The prophet outlines four aspects of God's judgment that show the perfect equilibrium of the divine attributes. We will look at one of these aspects each day this week.

How have you seen God receive glory because of His love and compassion? _____

How have you seen God receive glory because of His wrath and severity? _____

> "[God's] judgment is as essential to His glory as His love."
> —John MacArthur

Week of JUNE 20

God Is a God of Inflexible Justice

Justice is a legal term that describes the righteousness of divine government. God is a just God. His justice is as unchanging as any other aspect of His character. God cannot change His mind or lower His moral standards. His justice is inflexible; His holy nature demands that it be so.

Read the description of God in the margin with which Nahum introduces his prophecy in 1:2-3. These are powerful statements, giving us an unmistakable look into God's character.

Notice it says God is "jealous." As a child, I was troubled the first time I heard that, because I pictured jealousy as an unwholesome trait. But this speaks of a righteous jealousy unique to God. He is intolerant of unbelief, rebellion, disloyalty, or infidelity. He resents the insults and the indignities of people who worship anything or anyone besides Him. He demands to be given His rightful place above all else that we love or worship.

This truth is taught in the first of the Ten Commandments: "I am the Lord your God, who brought you out of the land of Egypt, out of the house of slavery. You shall have no other gods before Me" (Exod. 20:2-3).

The second commandment forbids idolatry and explicitly describes God as jealous: "You shall not make for yourself an idol, or any likeness of what is in heaven above or on the earth beneath or in the water under the earth. You shall not worship them or serve them; for I, the Lord your God, am a jealous God, visiting the iniquity of the fathers on the children, on the third and the fourth generations of those who hate Me" (vv. 4-5).

God's holy jealousy is so descriptive of who He is that He even takes the name "Jealous" as His own: "You shall not worship any other god, for the Lord, *whose name is Jealous,* is a jealous God" (Exod. 34:14, emphasis added). And in Deuteronomy 4:24 we read, "The Lord your God is a consuming fire, a jealous God."

The message is clear: God is jealous for His glory, and to disgrace His honor in any way—by worshiping a false God, or disobeying the true God, or simply failing to love Him with all the heart, soul, mind, and strength—

"A jealous and avenging God is the LORD; the LORD is avenging and wrathful. The LORD takes vengeance on His adversaries, and He reserves wrath for His enemies. The LORD is slow to anger and great in power, and the LORD will by no means leave the guilty unpunished" (Nah. 1:2-3).

If you desire to dig deeper...

What do you learn about God's jealousy from the following:
- **Deuteronomy 32:16-21**
- **1 Kings 14:22-23**
- **Psalm 78:58**
- **Zechariah 1:14-17**
- **Zechariah 8:2-3**
- **1 Corinthians 10:21-22**

is to incite the jealousy of God and incur His holy wrath. Simply because of who He is, God is perfectly righteous to be jealous of His glory and to be angry at those who denigrate or defame Him in any way.

Why do you think a Bible study that features God's love should give all this attention to God's jealousy?
_____

A Bible study on God's love should give attention to God's jealousy because God's jealousy is an expression of His love. Jealousy is possible only in a love relationship.

God is jealous because He loves. He is jealous when those who are the object of His lovingkindness are drawn away by sin and evil to worship other gods. He is jealous when those who ought to love Him defy Him and set their love on lesser objects.

Read 1 Corinthians 16:22 in your Bible. God's supreme jealousy is against whom? _____

Those who refuse love to the Lord Jesus Christ abide under God's curse—because He is jealous for His own Son. Thus God's love—particularly the Father's love for the Son—is inextricably linked to His holy jealousy. His love would actually be diminished if He relinquished His jealous anger.

Look again at Nahum's prophecy against Nineveh. Here we see that God's wrath—tempered by His great patience and loving-kindness for so many years—must inevitably give way to His avenging anger against sin. Notice the emphasis placed on divine vengeance in just the second verse of Nahum's prophecy: "A jealous and *avenging* God is the Lord; the Lord is avenging and wrathful. The Lord takes *vengeance* on His adversaries, and *He reserves wrath for His enemies*" (Nah. 1:2, emphasis added).

The repetition of this solemn concept gives the prophecy a tone that is both fearful and serious—and fittingly so. These are no idle threats. God is about to avenge His name against a wicked city that was once the recipient of His patience and compassion. Now Nineveh will find no mercy.

No one violates the glory and the honor of God, no one slights His Son, and no one attacks those He loves—then escapes His wrath. Nahum 1:3 simply says, "The Lord will by no means leave the guilty unpunished."

Week of JUNE 20

In verse 2 we read, "The Lord . . . is furious" (KJV). "Furious" is translated from two Hebrew words *(ba'al chemah)* that literally mean the Lord is "master of His anger." It speaks of a controlled fury—again, not a transient emotion, not a passion, but a fixed disposition. "God is angry with the wicked every day" (Ps. 7:11, KJV). His wrath is constant, unwavering—but it is a burning fury against all those who rebel against Him. "The Lord will by no means leave the guilty unpunished" (Nah. 1:3).

Sinners often presume on the mercy and goodness of God. He is slow to anger (v. 3)—patient, longsuffering, kind, and gracious. But no sinner should ever take the goodness of God for granted. No one should mistake His patience for weakness. No one should assume His kindness signifies permission to continue in sin and unbelief. No one should think of His love as an antidote to His wrath.

> "No sinner should ever take the goodness of God for granted."
> —John MacArthur

Do you take the goodness of God for granted?
❑ Yes   ❑ No

Read Romans 2:4 in your Bible. Circle the phrase that truthfully completes this statement:
• **God's goodness is given to:**
comfort sinners   or   to lead sinners to repentance.

Yet many do misinterpret God's goodness as apathy toward sin and a barrier to judgment. No one should miss the real point of God's longsuffering. Though loving, He has no plan to overlook the transgressions of the wicked. "The Lord knows how . . . to keep the unrighteous under punishment for the day of judgment" (2 Pet. 2:9). He is not slack concerning His promises; just longsuffering (3:9).

Read Nahum 1:3 again. What phrase does Nahum add to warn his readers not to confuse God's patience with impotence? _____

Those who believe they are safe from judgment because God has not yet poured out His wrath had better think again. His goodness is not weakness; and His forbearance is not indifference. "Vengeance is Mine, and retribution," says the Lord. "In due time their foot will slip; for the day of their calamity is near, and the impending things are hastening upon them" (Deut. 32:35). "The Lord will by no means leave the guilty unpunished" (Nah. 1:3).

God Is a God of Irresistible Power

Nahum's statement that God is "great in power" in 1:3 introduces the second of three aspects of divine judgment that he highlights.

Nahum's entire prophecy is a verbal display of the divine majesty and a paean to God's power. "In whirlwind and storm is His way, and clouds are the dust beneath His feet" (v. 3). Anyone familiar with the power of a cyclone understands the gist of this. Nahum is describing the majestic power of God's fury, and he uses three aspects of nature to make the point: God's power in the heavens, God's power over the waters, and God's power on the land.

In Psalm 19:1 David wrote, "The heavens are telling of the glory of God; and their expanse is declaring the work of His hands." The glory Nahum sees in the heavens is God's avenging power. God controls the whirlwinds, the storms, and the clouds (v. 3). Those natural wonders are not only displays of divine power, but frequently are employed as instruments of His judgment.

In Nahum's prophecy not only the heavens, but also the waters represent God's vengeance. When Nahum wrote, "He rebukes the sea and makes it dry; He dries up all the rivers. Bashan and Carmel wither; the blossoms of Lebanon wither," he was foretelling the doom of Israel's enemies. Bashan, Carmel, and Lebanon were the boundaries of Israel.

Nahum next spoke of God's power over the land: "Mountains quake because of Him, And the hills dissolve; Indeed the earth is upheaved by His presence, the world and all the inhabitants in it" (Nah. 1:5). God controls the earth. He can shake it whenever He likes. His power is irresistible.

Read the Scripture in the verses listed on the top of the next page. Draw a line matching each reference to the control it states God has over this earth.

Paean—a hymn of thanksgiving, a song of joy, triumph, or praise.

Why do you think Nahum used the lack of water to describe God's wrath against Assyria?

What are other ways you have seen water display God's power and/or wrath?

Week of JUNE 20

Psalm 97:5	He overturns mountains and crumbles cliffs.
Isaiah 64:3	The hills melt like hot wax before Him.
Ezekiel 38:20	The mountains quake at His presence.

In Nahum 1:6, the prophet asks, "Who can stand before His indignation? Who can endure the burning of His anger?" The answer is that *no one* can stand before Him. This is a description of divine judgment: "His wrath is poured out like fire, And the rocks are broken up by Him."

Divine wrath did finally bring about the doom of Nineveh, and all Nahum's prophecies were dramatically fulfilled.

God's justice is absolutely inflexible. His power is absolutely irresistible. Our God is a consuming fire. No wonder the writer of Hebrews gave us the warning he did in Hebrews 12:25-29.

God Is a God of Infinite Mercy

In verse 7 Nahum introduces a brief interlude into his prophecy of doom against the enemies of Jehovah.

Read Nahum's reminder to the people of Israel in the margin. Why do you think the Hebrews needed this reminder since God's message of wrath wasn't directed toward them? _____

"The LORD is good, a stronghold in the day of trouble, and He knows those who take refuge in Him" (Nah. 1:7).

The Hebrew word translated "take refuge in" conveys the idea of trusting, confiding in, and fleeing to for protection. It speaks of faith. Those who "take refuge in" the Lord are those who *believe in and trust* Him (emphasis added). In fact, the *King James Version* translates the verse like this: "The Lord is good, a stronghold in the day of trouble; and he knoweth them that trust in him."

The Lord—the Judge Himself—is a stronghold for those who seek refuge in Him by faith. Those words in a nutshell contain the entire gospel of justification by faith. The same God who threatens judgment against the wicked lovingly, compassionately invites sinful souls in despair to find their refuge in Him. He alone will be their haven, their stronghold, their protection from divine judgment.

Again we see that the love of God and His wrath are inextricably linked. It is impossible to study one without encountering the other. That is why Nahum places his accolade to the goodness and mercy of God in the midst of a passage about God's wrath. This verse is not a digression from his theme; it is at the heart of his message.

This juxtaposition of the wrath and goodness of God is frankly hard for many people to swallow. Liberal theology flatly denies that a God of wrath can also be loving. Others deny God's essential goodness. They see the effect of evil in the world—poverty, disease, human wretchedness, natural disasters, and other disorders—and they conclude that God is cruel or unloving—or even deny that He exists. They cannot envision that a sovereign being who is truly good would tolerate so much evil.

But Nahum knew God as both sovereign and good. There was no contradiction. The Lord is good; forty-one times in the Old Testament we are told that His mercy endures forever. Seven times we find the phrase, "The Lord is good."

> **Read Psalm 62:11-12 below and underline what David and Nahum both knew about God.**
>
> **Circle what you personally believe about God.**
>
> "One thing God has spoken, two things have I heard: that you, O God, are strong, and that you, O LORD, are loving. Surely you will reward each person according to what he has done" (Ps. 62:11-12, NIV).

Write the following Scripture references next to the statement each makes about God.

| Psalm 33:5 | Psalm 145:9 |
| Matthew 19:17 | John 10:11,14 |

_____ Only God is good.
_____ God's goodness and compassion are directed toward all of His creation.
_____ God's goodness is personified in Jesus, the Good Shepherd.
_____ The earth is full of God's unfailing love.

All creation speaks of God's essential goodness. Don't let the profundity of that truth escape you.

No one appreciates the goodness of God like those who seek their refuge in Him. They are the ones who know Him and love Him. They are

Week of JUNE 20

the ones on whom He has set His eternal love. They have fled to Him as their stronghold, and found mercy. They experience His goodness like no others. They appreciate His love like no one else.

"And He knows those who take refuge in Him" (v. 7). Does that mean the only people He knows about are the ones who trust Him? Certainly not. Remember that the word "know" and its cognates are often used in Scripture as synonyms for love. "Cain knew his wife" (Gen. 4:17, KJV). The expression speaks of the most intimate kind of love—in this case, the sexual union between a man and his wife. When Scripture says God "knows" those who take refuge in Him, it means He loves them with the deepest, most tender, and most personal affection. It describes the intimacy of divine love, which is unparalleled by any earthly kind of love.

God intimately loves those who trust in Him. The knowledge of that love is the greatest of all delights that can be experienced by the human heart.

The infinite love and mercy of God is displayed in the salvation of His people.

Describe how God has been a refuge for you.

How have you observed His goodness in that refuge?

Do you personally know the love of God through salvation? ❏ **Yes** ❏ **No**

If you answered No, turn to the inside cover to discover how you can turn to Christ in faith and seek refuge in Him.

God Is a God of Inconceivable Righteousness

Nahum 1:7 is a clear testimony that God is good to those who seek refuge in Him, but the Ninevites of Nahum's day would ultimately provide an object lesson of a different sort: "Whatever you devise against the Lord, He will make a complete end of it. Distress will not rise up twice" (1:9).

John MacARTHUR, JR.

Read Nahum 1:10-14 in your Bible. In the space below, list the judgments God pronounced He would bring upon Nineveh.

God's judgment does not negate His essential goodness. Nor does His goodness alter the severity of judgment. God is longsuffering. But when He finally must act in judgment, He makes a complete end of it. Hardened sinners should take note and tremble.

Nahum's message in verses 10-14 foretells the defeat of the Assyrians. God's righteous contempt for their evil works is evident in His pronouncement against them in these verses.

Like a field of tangled thorns, the Assyrians were fit only for burning. Like drunkards, they were defenseless. And like dry stubble, they were powerless to withstand the consuming flames of divine wrath. The phrase, "one who plotted evil against the Lord, a wicked counselor," seems to refer to Sennacherib. Against the entire nation and all their idolatrous gods, the Lord prophesied total destruction. The prophecy was fulfilled to the letter.

Read about the fulfillment of the prophecy in 2 Kings 19:35-37 in the margin.
Circle what God used to bring destruction to the Assyrian army.
Underline how God brought judgment to Sennacherib.

"Then it happened that night that the angel of the LORD went out and struck 185,000 in the camp of the Assyrians; and when men rose early in the morning, behold, all of them were dead. So Sennacherib king of Assyria departed and returned *home*, and lived at Nineveh. It came about as he was worshiping in the house of Nisroch his god, that Adrammelech [uh-DRAM-uh-lek] and Sharezer [shuh-REE-zuhr] killed him with the sword; and they escaped into the land of Ararat" (2 Kings 19:35-37, NASB).

But that was only the beginning of the judgment of the Assyrians—and of Nineveh in particular. Beginning in chapter 2, Nahum prophesies the destruction of Nineveh, a prophecy that was fulfilled exactly as it is recorded. After a series of enemy attacks and natural disasters, Nineveh was overwhelmed by the armies of the Medes, and the city was utterly leveled. When Nineveh fell, the Assyrian Empire toppled along with it.

Again we see that God's wrath is proof of His love. His judgment is linked to His faithfulness. And He is righteous when He judges. Nineveh was finished as a city. To this day the site lies in ruins, giving mute testimony to the severity of God's wrath against sin.

Read Nahum 3:19 and complete the following:
- Did Nineveh have any hope of escaping or recovering from God's judgment?   ☐ Yes   ☐ No
- How do you know that? _____
- How would the other nations respond to Nineveh's fall? _____
- Why? _____

Week of JUNE 20

God's severe judgment of Nineveh is also a reminder of God's immeasurable love for His own people. The destruction of Nineveh freed Israel from centuries of grief at the hands of marauding Assyrians. It was God's message to a wayward nation that He still loved them. God had chastened Israel severely for her sins. But His purpose in afflicting Israel was only corrective. Through Nahum, He assured them, "[The Assyrians] will be cut off and pass away. Though I have afflicted you, I will afflict you no longer" (1:12).

There is a vast and important difference between God's judgment and His discipline. Judgment is severe, final, destructive. Discipline is loving, tender, and corrective (Heb. 12:6). His discipline has a loving purpose (vv. 10-11). His judgment against the wicked, however, is of a different character altogether. To the wanton unbeliever, "Our God is a consuming fire" (v. 29). And again, "His calamity will come suddenly; Instantly he will be broken, and there will be no healing" (Prov. 6:15).

No one should be lulled into carelessness by the knowledge that God is loving and gracious. God's love is immeasurable, unfathomable, and inexhaustible. It is perfectly correct to say that God's love is infinite. But that does not mean His love negates His righteousness or overrules His holy wrath. Those who are not upright in heart—those who spurn God's love and follow their own ways—will ultimately suffer the same fate as Nineveh. That city, where the love of God was once poured out in so great abundance, finally perished in the fury of His wrath.

> "There is no relief for your breakdown, your wound is incurable. All who hear about you will clap their hands over you, for on whom has not your evil passed continually?"
> (Nah. 3:19, NASB).

> "My son, do not make light of the Lord's discipline, and do not lose heart when he rebukes you, because the Lord disciplines those he loves, and he punishes everyone he accepts as a son"
> (Heb. 12:5-6, NIV).

In all honesty, how do you feel about God's complete judgment of Nineveh?
___ **It seems so harsh.**
___ **They completely deserved it.**
___ **It makes me afraid of God.**
___ **It makes me thankful God is wrath and love because** _____

Amy SUMMERS

NOTES

To the Leader:

If you think it is difficult to teach a lesson about God's wrath, consider how Nahum must have felt having to deliver that pronouncement of doom!

Don't go into this lesson lightly. Pray over it daily. If possible, obtain commentaries and conduct your own personal study of Nahum.

Day 4 gives an opportunity for participants to escape God's judgment by accepting Christ. Be sensitive to notice those who may be contemplating that decision.

Before the Session

1. Read *During the Session*. Choose the teaching steps you will use in your teaching plan.
2. Secure two photographs—one displaying beauty and tranquility in nature, such as mountains or a lake; the other portraying the aftereffects of a natural disaster.
3. Enlist three volunteers to read: (1) Psalm 104:1-3,19-23; (2) Psalm 104:10-13; (3) Psalm 104:5,14.

During the Session

1. Welcome participants. Open with prayer requests and prayer.
2. Ask someone to read the lesson title for Day 1 for the week of June 6. [What is love?] Ask: *How did the apostle John answer that question?* [God is love.] *How did Jonah learn that truth in our study last week? How did God receive glory through His compassion to Nineveh?*
3. Display the photograph of a beautiful nature scene (or describe a tranquil setting if you were unable to secure photographs). Ask, *How does God receive glory through this beauty?* Display the photograph of a natural disaster. Ask: *How does God receive glory from this? When we attribute natural disasters to God's power are we just reinforcing the world's tendency to blame God for all bad things that happen? Explain your response.* Explain that this week's study can assist adults in determining how God receives glory through a demonstration of His severity as well as His compassion.
4. Request volunteers share their responses to the "grandfather" activity in Day 1 to determine how the Hebrews suffered under the Assyrians. Direct half the class to silently read 2 Kings 17:24,29-34 and the other half to read 2 Chronicles 28:19-25. After they have read, ask: *What was the worst thing to happen to the Hebrew people as a result of Assyrian oppression? We know Nineveh had at least one chance to repent, do you think by now they had used up all their chances? Why, or why not?*
5. Read aloud Nahum 1:2-6. Inquire: *What is the first thing we learn about God from Nahum? Does it disturb you that God is described as*

Week of JUNE 20

jealous? *Why, or why not?* Request volunteers look up and read the Scripture references listed in the margin in Day 2. Work together as a class to determine the reasons for God's jealousy. Compare God's jealousy to human jealousy. Ask, *How is God's jealousy an expression of His love?*

6. Write "heavens, waters, and land" on the board. Ask participants to state how God would use each aspect of nature to judge Nineveh. Write responses on the board. Remind the class that although you are focusing on God's severity, you must never lose sight of His goodness. Request the volunteers read their verses from Psalm 104 and guide the class to state how God uses the same three aspects of nature to show His goodness. Write responses on the board.

7. Read Nahum 1:7. Ask why the Hebrew people needed a reminder of God's goodness (first activity of Day 4). Allow volunteers to share how they have known God's goodness as He has been a refuge for them.

8. Ask how the final verse of Nahum predicts the Ninevites would not be able to find refuge in God this time. Request learners read Nahum 2:5,13 and 3:13 and state what would happen to Nineveh's military might. Direct them to scan 2:5-6 and 3:12-15 and declare the fate of Nineveh's fortresses and walls. Request they read 2:9-10 and 3:5-6 and tell what would happen to Nineveh's wealth and pride. Read aloud Nahum 3:1-3 to discover what would happen to its inhabitants. Ask: *After Nineveh experienced all this calamity, how do you think the few survivors might have answered Nahum's question in 1:6—"Who can endure the burning of His anger?" How would many people today answer that question?*

9. Ask, *Now that we are aware of God's severity—what are we to do?* Request someone read Hebrews 12:25-29. Lead a discussion with these questions: *What will receive the final shaking? What will be destroyed? What will remain?*

10. Discuss how today's lesson has helped participants understand how God is glorified through His severity as well as His compassion.

11. Close in prayer.

After the Session

1. Encourage participants who have questions about receiving salvation to speak with you or your pastor this week.
2. Read next week's lesson and complete the learning activities.

NOTES

John MacArthur, Jr.

Asking Hard Questions

day One

Disturbing Questions

Jesus loves me, this I know,
For the Bible tells me so.

From childhood most of us have heard that God loves us. The Bible tells us that love is at the very heart of who God is: *"God is love"* (1 John 4:8,16, emphasis added) and He is "the God of love and peace" (2 Cor. 13:11).

In your opinion, why should the truth taught in those verses be among the first things we teach our children about God?

But don't get the idea that God's love is only a child's subject. And don't think that you have mastered the subject by absorbing what you were taught as a child. This subject is certainly *not* child's play. God's love raises some very complex and sometimes disturbing questions: If God is love, why is the world such a theater of tragedy? If God is so loving, why does He allow His own people to suffer? If "God so loved the world"—then why does He allow all the suffering and torture and pain and sorrow and grief and death? If God is both loving and omnipotent, then why is the world such a mess? Why would a loving God ever allow wars and famines and disasters to cause so much human anguish? If God is the loving Father of humanity, why doesn't He act like a human father who loves his children? Why does He allow His creatures to make choices that result in their destruction, when He could prevent it or overrule it? If God is a loving God, why did He allow sin in the first place, and why death?

Week of JUNE 27

There are more questions, and they get even harder: If God is love, why isn't everyone saved? Why would a loving God send people to hell to suffer forever? Why would a loving God devise a plan that has so many people going to hell for all eternity? What kind of love is it that can control the world but allows the world to suffer the way it suffers? What kind of love is it that is sovereign and yet sends poor, suffering people to an eternal flame? How are we to understand that kind of love?

Read the following Scriptures and record the question asked of God.
Judges 6:13 _____
Job 9:12 _____
Lamentations 5:20 _____
Mark 4:35-38 _____

How do you feel reading such questions presented to God? (check one and complete the statement)
❑ It makes me uncomfortable because... _____
❑ It makes me angry because... _____
❑ It comforts me because... _____
❑ Other? _____

If you desire to dig deeper...

Read the following passages and record the "why" questions asked of God. Star the questions you have asked God.

• Genesis 25:22
• Numbers 11:11
• Deuteronomy 29:24
• Psalm 10:1
• Psalm 44:23-24
• Jeremiah 14:19
• Jeremiah 15:18

Wrong Answers to the Hard Questions About God's Love

Those difficult questions are reasonable, and they need to be faced honestly. It won't do to pretend such difficulties are easy to answer, or simply ignore them and hope they go away. Anyone who thinks deeply about God will eventually come face-to-face with those very questions and others like them. They are unsettling, vexing, even bewildering questions. Genuinely satisfying answers to them are elusive. There's no point in pretending such questions should pose no problems for the Christian.

In fact, history reveals that those who settle for easy answers to these questions often make shipwreck of the faith. Usually they will cite Scripture selectively and ignore half of some important biblical truth while grossly overemphasizing the other half. And so they tend to go to extremes.

Universalism, for example, teaches that in the end everyone will be saved. Universalists believe that because God is love, He cannot eternally condemn anyone. In the end, they believe, hell will not even exist. Some teach that the devil and his fallen angels will be redeemed.

Another attempt to solve the dilemma posed by God's love is a theory known as *annihilationism.* Under this scheme, God takes believers to heaven and puts the rest out of existence. They experience no conscious punishment or suffering; they are judged by having their existence terminated. According to this view, therefore, there is no such place as eternal hell.

A doctrine closely related to annihilationism is a theory known as *conditional immortality.* This view suggests that the human soul is transient until immortality is bestowed upon it. Since eternal life is given only to believers, all others simply pass into oblivion after the final judgment.

Those views may serve to salve human emotion to some degree, but they don't do justice to what Scripture teaches. Therefore, they are errors—and extremely dangerous ones at that, because they give people a false sense of safety. Jesus Himself described hell in graphic terms. In fact, He had more to say about hell than anyone else in Scripture.

Read Jesus' teachings in Matthew 8:12; 13:42; Mark 9:43-48; and Luke 13:28. In two or three sentences, explain what Jesus wanted people to know about hell.

_____

_____

Furthermore, Revelation 14:11 describes hell's torments as unremitting and eternal: "The smoke of their torment goes up forever and ever; and they have no rest day and night." Revelation 20:10 states, "They will be tormented day and night forever and ever." Matthew 25:46 says, "These [unbelievers] will go away into eternal punishment, but the righteous into

Week of JUNE 27

eternal life." That verse employs the same Greek word for "eternal" (*aionios*—meaning "perpetual, everlasting, forever") to describe both the bliss of heaven and the punishments of hell.

Embracing any of these theories also usually has the effect of making people indifferent to evangelism. They begin to feel comfortable that everyone will either be saved or put out of misery, so evangelism loses its urgency. The gospel seems less compelling. And that is precisely the effect these theories have had in churches and denominational groups where they have been espoused.

But one can easily err in the other direction as well. Some Christians who ponder the hard questions about divine love conclude that God simply does not love people who aren't His own; He hates them. Under this scheme, there's no tension between the love of God and His wrath. There's no reason to wonder how God can love people whom He ultimately condemns, because you simply conclude that whoever He condemns He hates. Persons who hold this view conclude that such hatred and genuine love are mutually exclusive.

Read Psalm 5:4-5; Proverbs 6:16-19; and Romans 9:13. How might people who hold this incorrect view of God use these verses to support their position?

_____

That view doesn't do justice to Scripture. It restricts God's love to a remnant, and pictures Him hating the vast majority of humanity. In terms of sheer numbers, it suggests that God's hatred for humanity overwhelms His love. That is not consistent with the God of Scripture.

Read Exodus 34:6 and Nehemiah 9:17. In the margin, list the descriptions of God found in those verses.

Read Psalm 145:8-9. To whom does God display the characteristics you listed in the margin? _____

And what about "God so loved the world" (John 3:16)? The whole point of verse 17 is to assert that Christ's advent was a search-and-rescue mission, not a crusade for judgment: "For God did not send the Son into the world to judge the world, but that the world should be saved through

Him" (v. 17). The point is that God's primary purpose in sending Christ was born out of love, not a design to condemn. Christ's purpose in coming was to save, not to destroy. Titus 3:4 also speaks of God's love: "The kindness of God our Savior and His *love for mankind* appeared" (emphasis added).

The Right Approach

How then shall we answer the hard questions about divine love? One other solution is often suggested. It is to tell those inclined to ask hard questions, "Shut your mouth. You have no right to ask the question." People who take this approach will point to Romans 9:20-21, where the apostle Paul replied to a skeptic of God's sovereignty by saying:

> On the contrary, who are you, O man, who answers back to God? The thing molded will not say to the molder, "Why did you make me like this," will it? Or does not the potter have a right over the clay, to make from the same lump one vessel for honorable use, and another for common use?

Take a few moments to learn some lessons from a potter's workshop. Read the following Scriptures and answer the questions.

Isaiah 64:8:
Who is the Potter? _____
Who is the clay? _____

Isaiah 29:16:
What happens when the pot forgets who is the created and Who is the Creator? _____

Isaiah 45:9-12:
How does the Potter respond to the pot that is unhappy with His handiwork? _____

Week of JUNE 27

**Jeremiah 18:1-6:
What determines the shape into which the clay is formed?** _____

Who are we to question God? That is what Paul asks in Romans 9:20-21. God is God. He will do whatever He wants to do because He is completely sovereign. He is the Potter. He decides what the pot will be like. And the pot has no right to object.

Obviously, that is all very true. God is God. We cannot comprehend His ways. Many of the questions we ask have answers we could never comprehend. Certainly we have no right to challenge God's motives. We are not entitled to subject Him to our interrogation, as if He were accountable to us. And sometimes the questions we raise do not even deserve to be answered. In the end, we will be left with many unanswered questions. That will bring us to Romans 9:20 and the inevitable place where we must simply close our mouths and stand in awe.

But before we get to that point, there are many things that we do need to understand. Romans 9:20 is a fitting response to a skeptic. It is appropriate for the person who will not be satisfied with knowing what God Himself has revealed. But for the truth-seeker sincerely wanting to understand God and His love, there is much in the Bible to help him come to grips with the hard questions before coming to a stop at Romans 9:20.

"Many of the questions we ask have answers we could never comprehend."
—John MacArthur

Read Psalm 46:10. What is the appropriate response when you finally realize you will not receive an answer to your hard question about God and His ways?

_____

That is not to say that we can find all the answers to our hardest questions. We can't. Sometimes God Himself does not reveal to us the answers to those questions. Anyone who pretends to know more than God has told us is foolish.

Ultimately we reach the place where we must leave our questions to God and trust His essential righteousness, His lovingkindness, His tender mercy, and His justice. We learn to live with the *unanswered* questions in light of what we *know* to be true about God. At that point, Romans 9:20

becomes a satisfying answer, because we know we can trust the Potter. Meanwhile, as we search God's Word with an open heart, God's own self-revelation gives us a wonderful, marvelous, rich, comprehensible understanding of His love.

What do you know to be true about God? _____

_____

How does that help you live with unanswered questions? _____

Wrong Questions Based on a Wrong Perspective of God

In grappling with the hard questions about God's love it is crucial to bear in mind that human tendency to see things from the wrong perspective. We cannot comprehend an infinite God with our finite minds. If we attempt to measure God from a human perspective, all our thinking about Him will be out of whack. And we sin against God when we think things of Him that are unbefitting of His glory.

According to Psalm 50:21 who does God rebuke?
- ❑ People who question Him.
- ❑ People who underestimate Him by thinking of Him in human terms.
- ❑ People who get angry with Him.

Remember how the book of Job ends? After all Job's suffering, and his friends' counsel that actually added to his sufferings, God rebuked not only Job's counselors, but also Job himself, for entertaining thoughts about God that were not sufficiently high. Both Job and his counselors were attempting to explain God in human terms. They were trying

Week of JUNE 27

to make sense of what Job was going through, but their failure to see God as far above His creatures had skewed their view of what was happening. The counselors were giving the wrong answers, and Job was asking the wrong questions. God put some questions of His own to Job.

Read Job 38:2-13.

I love that portion of Scripture! God is recounting His own creative works, and asking if Job is wise enough to tell God how these things are to be done. From this point on, for three or four chapters, God lists the marvels of His creation and challenges Job to tell Him if he knows better than God how the universe ought to be run. Rather than seeking to vindicate Himself in Job's eyes, God simply appealed to His own sovereignty: "Will the faultfinder contend with the Almighty? Let him who reproves God answer it" (40:1).

Read Job 40:4-5. What physical posture depicts Job's response to God's questions? (Check)
- ❑ Hands clutching head
- ❑ Hand over mouth
- ❑ Hands tightly clenched at side

What did that posture signify? _____

Then God asked Job, "Will you really annul My judgment? *Will you condemn Me that you may be justified?* Or do you have an arm like God, and can you thunder with a voice like His?" (40:8-9; emphasis added). Job's questions, valid as they may have seemed for someone who had suffered all Job had suffered, actually cast aspersions on God's character. Job was stepping over the line if he thought he could justify himself at God's expense.

Job, by God's own testimony, was a blameless and upright man. There was no one like Job on the face of the earth (1:8). Yet he suffered—probably more than anyone else had ever suffered. Job was not as deserving of such suffering as anyone else would have been. Why was he taking the brunt of so much catastrophe? Where was God's love and His sense of justice and fair play? It was inevitable that Job would struggle with some very difficult questions like those, as people do today.

> "Why did I not perish at birth, and die as I came from the womb?" (Job 3:11, NIV).
>
> "What strength do I have, that I should still hope? What prospects, that I should be patient?" (Job 6:11, NIV).
>
> "Will you never look away from me, or let me alone even for an instant? If I have sinned, what have I done to you, O watcher of men? Why have you made me your target? Have I become a burden to you? Why do you not pardon my offenses and forgive my sins?" (Job 7:19-21a, NIV).
>
> ("Does it please you to oppress me, to spurn the work of your hands, while you smile on the schemes of the wicked? Do you have eyes of flesh? Do you see as a mortal sees?" (Job 10:3-4, NIV).
>
> "How many wrongs and sins have I committed? Show me my offense and my sin" (Job 13:23, NIV).
>
> "Why does the Almighty not set times for judgment? Why must those who know him look in vain for such days?" (Job 24:1, NIV).

But the moment Job's questions reflected misgivings about God—His wisdom, His love, His goodness, and the equity of His justice—Job and his friends had crossed the line. They were appraising God by human standards. They forgot that God is the Potter and we are merely the clay. So God rebuked them.

Read the passages from Job in the margin. Draw a star next to the questions you think crossed the line from questioning God's actions to questioning God's character.

Job immediately saw his sin: "Therefore I have declared that which I did not understand, things too wonderful for me, which I did not know" (42:3).

We need to bear in mind as we ponder the love and the wrath of God that in many ways these things touch on knowledge "too wonderful" for us. "It is too high, [we] cannot attain to it" (Ps. 139:6). God confronts us with the same kinds of questions He asked Job.

Read Isaiah 40:13-14; Romans 11:34; and 1 Corinthians 2:16 in your Bible. Next to each question below, write the Scripture passage that asks that question.

Who knows God's mind? _____

Who is God's counselor? _____

Who shows God the right way? _____

Who enlightens God with knowledge and understanding? _____

Who is God's instructor? _____

What is the only answer to each question? _____

As we ponder our own hard questions about God's love, we must take great care lest the very questions themselves provoke us to think inadequate or inappropriate thoughts about God or develop sinful attitudes toward His love and wisdom.

Week of JUNE 27

Wrong Inferences from a Faulty View of Divine Providence

We dare not make the error Job's counselors made, thinking we can observe the workings of providence and thereby discern the mind of God. Job's friends thought his sufferings were proof that Job was guilty of some secret sin. In reality, the opposite was true. Since it is clear from many scriptures that we cannot know God's mind, we must not try to read too much into His works of providence.

By that, I mean we cannot assume we know the meaning or purpose of every fortune or disaster that befalls.

Read the Scriptures in the margin. What hard question is common to all four passages?

_____

What often seems like divine blessing is no proof of God's favor. Don't think for a moment that prosperity is proof of divine approval. Those who think in those terms are prone to go astray.

On the other hand, the righteous frequently suffer: "Indeed, all who desire to live godly in Christ Jesus will be persecuted" (2 Tim. 3:12). "Unto you it is given in the behalf of Christ, not only to believe on him, but also to suffer for his sake" (Phil. 1:29). But God uses such suffering to accomplish much good: "God causes all things to work together for good to those who love God" (Rom. 8:28).

In other words, the very thing that seems good will end in evil for the impenitent and unbelieving.

Read Genesis 50:20 in the margin of the next page and fill in the blank. Whenever trouble comes to one of God's children, that believer can state with confidence, "You intended this for evil, but God _____."

"The tents of the destroyers prosper, and those who provoke God are secure, whom God brings into their power" (Job 12:6, NASB).

"I have seen a violent, wicked man spreading himself like a luxuriant tree in its native soil" (Ps. 37:35, NASB).

"Behold, these are the wicked; and always at ease, they have increased in wealth" (Ps. 73:12, NASB).

"Righteous art Thou, O LORD, that I would plead my case with Thee; Indeed I would discuss matters of justice with Thee: Why has the way of the wicked prospered? Why are all those who deal in treachery at ease?" (Jer. 12:1, NASB).

53

> "As for you, you meant evil against me, but God meant it for good in order to bring about this present result, to preserve many people alive"
> (Gen. 50:20, NASB).

Therefore, the greatest disaster from our perspective may actually be a token of God's lovingkindness.

Clearly, we cannot know the mind of God. There are, therefore, many pitfalls to avoid in both asking and answering the hard questions about God's love. The subject is not child's play. With those things in mind, we can delve into what God Himself reveals in His Word—and surely we will find that it is a very fruitful study.

Based on your study of this week's lesson, what are the pitfalls you must avoid in asking the hard questions about divine love? (Review each day's study if necessary.)

_____
_____
_____

Have you ever fallen into any of the pitfalls you listed?

❏ Yes   ❏ No   ❏ Not Sure

What have you gained from this week's study that will help you avoid those pitfalls in the future?

_____
_____
_____

Week of JUNE 27

NOTES

Before the Session
1. Read *During the Session*. Choose the teaching steps you will use in your teaching plan.

During the Session
1. Welcome participants. Open with prayer requests and prayer.
2. Invite participants to recite (or sing if you have a brave class) the children's hymn "Jesus Loves Me." Ask: *Why is teaching a child about God's love the greatest gift you can offer? How does the foundational awareness of God's love sustain us when, as adults, we are bombarded with hard questions about divine love?*
3. Ask volunteers to share which of the questions voiced in Day 1 they have heard others ask. Request volunteers look up and read the Scriptures listed in the margin in Day 1. Ask: *Are you surprised to hear so many people asking God "why?" Why? How were these biblical personalities expressing trust even as they asked hard questions? How do you think God feels about us asking Him these questions? Why?* Request a volunteer read Psalm 22:1. Ask participants if they can recall who else asked that question. Read aloud Matthew 27:46. Ask: *Does the fact that even Jesus asked God "Why?" change your attitude about asking God difficult questions? Explain.*
4. From Day 2, ask participants to name and explain the wrong answers people give to the hard questions about God's love.[universalism, annihilationism, conditional immortality] Ask: *How have you encountered these mindsets? Why are they wrong?* [They give people a false sense of safety. They make people indifferent to evangelism. They state God only loves His own and hates everyone else. They suggest God's hatred overwhelms His love.] To combat these wrong teachings, request learners state what Jesus taught about hell (first activity in Day 2). Ask adults to use the characteristics of God they listed in the final activity of Day 2 to refute the incorrect view that God hates those He condemns.

To the Leader:

Carefully read Job 38–41. How do these chapters humble you as a teacher of God's Word? How do they encourage you? As you determine questions to ask your class this week, be sensitive to the questions God is asking you. Spend time in silence in God's presence before you even think about speaking about Him before your class.

NOTES

5. Ask, *If those are wrong approaches to hard questions, what is the right approach?* Ask someone to read Romans 9:20-21. Ask how learners reconcile that truth with the idea that it is all right to ask questions of God. Ask: *If it is OK to ask hard questions, where should we go for the right answers? What must we do if the answers do not come?* Allow volunteers to share their responses to the final activity of Day 3.

6. Ask, *When does questioning God turn to sin?* Request volunteers read Job's questions in the margin of Day 4. Discuss which questions participants think crossed the line from reasonable to irreverent and why. It's OK if adults disagree; allow the discussion to convict and challenge.

7. Read aloud Job 38:1-3. Comment: *Job had been doing all the questioning. Who was doing the asking now?* Ask those who completed this week's study to share what they liked or disliked about God's questioning of Job in 38:4-13. Explain that God's questions of Job continue for three more chapters. Request a volunteer read Job's final response in Job 42:1-6. Ask volunteers who have had an experience with God similar to this account to relate that encounter and explain how it changed their view of themselves and God. Be prepared to share from your own experience if necessary.

8. Direct adults to answer "No one" out loud after you read each of the five questions in the final activity of Day 4. Discuss how that truth can ultimately help learners accept unanswered hard questions of life.

9. Ask adults to share the most burning, difficult question they have about God's love. Read aloud the quotation from the margin in Day 3. ("Many of the questions we ask have answers we could never comprehend.") Ask: *How could someone use that truth as an excuse to not put forth the effort to seek godly answers? How can that truth be a statement of faith?* Discuss the final activity of Day 5.

10. Close in prayer, thanking God that participants can trust His goodness and love even when difficult questions go unanswered.

After the Session

1. Read next week's lesson and complete the learning activities.
2. Be sensitive to participants who are struggling with difficult questions about God's love. Schedule a time to meet with them this week to help them grapple with tough questions while still grasping God's love for them.

Week of JULY 4

The Love of God for Humanity

John 3:16

If you can, write John 3:16 from memory. _____

_____

_____

John 3:16 may be the most familiar verse in all of Scripture, but it is surely one of the most abused and least understood. "God so loved the world" has become a favorite cheer for many people who presume on God's love and who do not love Him in return. The verse is often quoted as evidence that God loves everyone and that He is infinitely merciful—as if the verse negated all the biblical warnings of condemnation for the wicked.

That is not the point of John 3:16. One has only to read verse 18 to see the balance of the truth.

Read John 3:18. What is the flip side to the truth that those who believe in Christ will not be condemned?

_____

Surely this is a truth that needs to be proclaimed to the world at least as urgently as the truth of John 3:16.

Nevertheless, while acknowledging that some people are prone to abuse the notion of God's love, we cannot respond by minimizing what Scripture says about the extent of God's love. John 3:16 is a rich and crucial verse. John 3:16 is a statement about God's demeanor toward mankind in general. It is a declaration of *good* news, and its point is to say that Christ came into the world on a mission of salvation, not a mission of condemnation: "For God did not send the Son into the world to judge the world, but that the world should be saved through Him" (v. 17).

Take a fresh look at John 3:16 and try to absorb the real sense of it.

God so loved what? _____
Describe the world that God loved. _____

God loved that world of humanity so much that He gave what? _____
Why did God make such a great sacrifice? _____

The end result of God's love is therefore the gospel message—the free offer of life and mercy to anyone who believes. In other words, the gospel—an indiscriminate offer of divine mercy to everyone without exception—manifests God's compassionate love and unfeigned lovingkindness to all humanity.

What new insights did you gain into John 3:16 as a result of today's study? _____

Does God Really Love People He Does Not Save?

Mark 10 relates a familiar story that illustrates God's love for the lost. It is the account of the rich young ruler who came to Jesus and asked Him a great question.

Read Mark 10:17. What did the young man want to know? _____

Week of JULY 4

Scripture tells us:

> And Jesus said to him, "Why do you call Me good? No one is good except God alone. You know the commandments, 'Do not murder, Do not commit adultery, Do not steal, Do not bear false witness, Do not defraud, Honor your father and mother'" (vv. 18-19).

Read John 14:6. What did Jesus declare was the only way to God? _____
Then why do you think Jesus quoted the Law in response to the young man's question? _____
_____

Every aspect of Jesus' reply was designed to confront the young man's sin. Jesus' reply to this young man had a twofold purpose: first, to underscore His own deity, confronting the young man with the reality of who He was; and second, to gently chide a brash young man who clearly thought of *himself* as good.

To stress this second point, Jesus quoted a section of the Decalogue. Had the young man been genuinely honest with himself, he would have had to admit that he had not kept the law perfectly. But instead, he responded confidently, "Teacher, I have kept all these things from my youth up" (v. 20). This was unbelievable impertinence on the young man's part. It shows how little he understood of the demands of the law. This rich young ruler was not even willing to admit he had sinned.

> The *Decalogue* refers to the Ten Commandments.

Read Mark 10:21-22. What was the second test Jesus gave the young man? _____
Why would Jesus demand so much of this young man? _____
Circle the grade you think the young man made on this "test"?
    A+   B   C-   D   F

There were two things he refused to do: he would not acknowledge his sin, and he would not bow to Christ's lordship. In other words, he shut himself off from the eternal life he seemed so earnestly to be seeking. As it turned out, there were things more important to him than eternal life, after all. His pride and his personal property took priority in his heart over the claims of Christ on his life. And so he turned away from the only true Source of the life he thought he was seeking.

That is the last we ever see of this man in the New Testament. As far as the biblical record is concerned, he remained in unbelief.

**What significant phrase about Jesus' regard for this young man is tucked away in verse 21? _____
What do you think is the importance of that phrase?**

_____

How Is God's Universal Love Manifested?

God's love is manifest universally to all people in at least four ways.

COMMON GRACE
Common grace is a term theologians use to describe the goodness of God to all mankind universally. Common grace restrains sin and the effects of sin on the human race. Common grace is what keeps humanity from descending into the morass of evil that we would see if the full expression of our fallen nature were allowed to have free reign.

Scripture teaches that we are tainted with sin in every aspect of our being (Rom. 3:10-18). Human nature is corrupt: "There is none righteous, not even one" (Rom. 3:10). "The heart is more deceitful than all else and is desperately sick" (Jer. 17:9). Unregenerate men and women are "dead in . . . trespasses and sins" (Eph. 2:1). All people are by nature "foolish . . . disobedient, deceived, enslaved to various lusts and pleasures, spending [their lives] in malice" (Titus 3:3). This is true of all alike, "For all have sinned and fall short of the glory of God" (Rom. 3:23).

Common grace is all that restrains the full expression of human sinfulness.

Week of JULY 4

Read the following Scriptures. Draw a line matching each passage to the truth it states about God's goodness to all humanity.

Psalm 50:1-2	God maintains order in human society through government.
Matthew 5:45	God enables humans to admire beauty and goodness.
Romans 2:15	God imparts blessings indiscriminately on the righteous and the unrighteous.
Romans 13:1-5	God gives everyone a conscience.

Common grace *ought* to be enough to move sinners to repentance. The apostle Paul rebukes the unbeliever: "Do you think lightly of the riches of His kindness and forbearance and patience, not knowing that the kindness of God leads you to repentance?" (Rom. 2:4). Yet because of the depth of depravity in the human heart, sinners spurn the goodness of God.

Common grace does not pardon sin or redeem sinners, but it is nevertheless a sincere token of God's goodwill to mankind in general. As the apostle Paul said, "In Him we live and move and exist . . . for we also are His offspring" (Acts 17:28). That takes in everyone on earth, not just those whom God adopts as sons. God deals with us all as His offspring, people made in His image: "The Lord is good to all, and His mercies are over all His works" (Ps. 145:9).

When we understand that all of humanity is fallen and rebellious and unworthy of any blessing from God's hand, it helps give a better perspective: "Because of the Lord's great love we are not consumed, for His compassions never fail" (Lam. 3:22, NIV). And the only reason God ever gives us anything to laugh at, smile at, or enjoy is because He is a good and loving God. If He were not, we would be immediately consumed by His wrath.

Acts 14 contains a helpful description of common grace. Here Paul and Barnabas were ministering at Lystra, when Paul healed a lame man. The crowds saw it and someone began saying that Barnabas was Zeus and Paul was Hermes. The priest at the local temple of Zeus wanted to organize a sacrifice to them.

Read Paul and Barnabas' response in Acts 14:14-17. What evidences of common grace do they mention in an attempt to direct the people's devotion to God?

That is a fine description of common grace. While allowing sinners to "go their own ways," God nevertheless bestows on them temporal tokens of His goodness and lovingkindness. It is not saving grace. It has no redemptive effect. Nevertheless, it is a genuine and unfeigned manifestation of divine lovingkindness to all people.

Compassion

God's love to all humanity is a love of *compassion*. To say it another way, it is a love of pity. It is a broken-hearted love. He is "good, and ready to forgive, and abundant in lovingkindness to all who call upon [Him]" (Ps. 86:5). "To the Lord our God belong compassion and forgiveness, for we have rebelled against Him" (Dan. 9:9). He is "compassionate and gracious, slow to anger, and abounding in lovingkindness and truth" (Exod. 34:6).

Again, we must understand that there is nothing in any sinner that compels God's love. He does not love us because we are lovable. He is not merciful to us because we in any way deserve His mercy. We are despicable, vile sinners who if we are not saved by the grace of God will be thrown on the trash heap of eternity, which is hell. We have no intrinsic value, no intrinsic worth—there's nothing in us to love.

I recently overheard a radio talk-show psychologist attempting to give a caller an ego-boost: "God loves you for what you are. You *must* see yourself as someone special. After all, you are special to God."

But that misses the point entirely. God *does not* love us "for what we are." He loves us *in spite of what we are*. He does not love us because we are special. Rather, it is only His love and grace that give our lives any significance at all. That may seem like a doleful perspective to those raised in a culture where self-esteem is elevated to the supreme virtue. But it is, after all, precisely what Scripture teaches: "We have sinned like our fathers, we have committed iniquity, we have behaved wickedly" (Ps. 106:6). "All of us have become like one who is unclean, and all our righteous deeds are like a filthy garment; and all of us wither like a leaf, and our iniquities, like the wind, take us away" (Isa. 64:6).

> "God does not love us for what we are. He loves us in spite of what we are"
> —John MacArthur

Week of JULY 4

God loves because He is love; love is essential to who He is. Rather than viewing His love as proof of something worthy in us, we ought to be humbled by it.

God's love for sinners is not the love of value; it is the love of pity for that which *could* have had value and has none. It is a love of compassion. It is a love of sorrow. It is a love of pathos. It is not a love that is incompatible with revulsion, but it is a genuine, well-meant, compassionate, sympathetic love nonetheless.

> **Read the following Scriptures. What emotions do you sense in each expression of love? For whom is that kind of love expressed and why?**
> **Isaiah 16:11-13** _____
> **Jeremiah 48:35-37** _____
> **Matthew 23:37** _____
> **Luke 19:41-44** _____

These words of doom were spoken in great sorrow. This sorrow is genuine sorrow, borne out of the heart of a divine Savior who "wanted to gather [them] together, the way a hen gathers her chicks under her wings," but they were "unwilling."

Further Ways God's Universal Love Is Manifested

ADMONITION

God's universal love is revealed not only in common grace and His great compassion, but also in His *admonition to repent*. God is constantly warning sinners of their impending fate, and pleading with them to turn away from sin. Nothing demonstrates God's love more than the various warnings throughout the pages of Scripture, urging sinners to flee from the wrath to come.

Anyone who knows anything about Scripture knows it is filled with warnings about the judgment to come, warnings about hell, and warnings about the severity of divine punishment. If God really did *not* love sinners, nothing would compel Him to warn them. He would be perfectly just to punish them for their sin and unbelief with no admonition whatsoever. But He *does* love and He *does* care and He does warn.

What are common warnings given to children?

_____

How are these warnings indications of love?

_____

Sometimes the warnings of Scripture bear the marks of divine wrath. They sound severe. They reflect God's hatred of sin. They warn of the irreversible condemnation that will befall sinners. They are unsettling, unpleasant, even terrifying. But they are admonitions from a loving God who weeps over the destruction of the wicked. They are necessary expressions from the heart of a compassionate Creator who takes no pleasure in the death of the wicked. They are further proof that God is love.

THE GOSPEL OFFER

Finally, we see proof that God's love extends to all in *the gospel offer*. Earlier we noted that the gospel invitation is an offer of divine mercy. Now consider the unlimited breadth of the offer. No one is excluded from the gospel invitation. Salvation in Christ is freely and indiscriminately offered to all.

Jesus told a parable in Matthew 22:2-14 about a king who was having a marriage celebration for his son.

Read Matthew 22:1-14 and complete the following:
How many times did the king summon the invited guests? _____
What inexcusable behavior did the summoned guests display? _____
What happened to them as a result? _____
Who ended up attending the king's banquet? _____
Write Jesus' conclusion to this parable. _____

Week of JULY 4

The parable represents God's dealing with the nation of Israel. They were the invited guests. But they rejected the Messiah. They spurned Him and mistreated Him and crucified Him. They wouldn't come—as Jesus said to them, "You search the Scriptures, because you think that in them you have eternal life; and it is these that bear witness of Me; and *you are unwilling to come to Me,* that you may have life" (John 5:39-40).

The gospel invites many to come who are unwilling to come. Many are called who are not chosen. The invitation to come is given indiscriminately to all. Whosoever will may come.

God's love for mankind does not stop with a warning of the judgment to come. It also invites sinners to partake of divine mercy. It offers forgiveness and mercy.

"Come to Me, all who are weary and heavy-laden, and I will give you rest. Take My yoke upon you, and learn from Me, for I am gentle and humble in heart; and you shall find rest for your souls" (Matt. 11:28-29, NASB).

Read Matthew 11:28-29 and John 6:37 in the margin. Circle what Jesus promised to those who would come to Him.

Great riches   Acceptance   Power   Rest

"The one who comes to Me I will certainly not cast out" (John 6:37, NASB).

It should be evident from these verses that the gospel is a *free offer* of Christ and His salvation to all who hear. God's love extends to the whole world. It covers all humanity. We see it in common grace. We see it in His compassion. We see it in His admonitions to the lost. And we see it in the free offer of the gospel to all.

God *is* love, and His mercy is over all His works.

How have you personally experienced God's love through:
His common grace? _____
_____
His compassion? _____
_____
His warnings? _____
_____
His free offer of the gospel? _____
_____

day Five

God's Love for His Own

God loves all humanity. But it is even more crucial that we see that God has a special love for *His own*, and that He loves them with an eternal, unchanging love.

John 13:1 describes the love of Christ for His disciples: "Having loved His own who were in the world, He loved them to the end." Another version translates that same verse this way: "Having loved his own who were in the world, he now showed them the full extent of his love" (NIV).

That little phrase "to the end" is an important phrase. The Greek expression is *eis telos*. "To the end" is an acceptable translation, but idiomatically this is an expression that carries the meaning "completely, perfectly, fully, or comprehensively—to the uttermost."

God loves the world, but He loves "His own" perfectly, unchangingly, completely, fully, comprehensively—*eis telos*. Let me say it simply: He loves His own to the complete extent of His capacity to love His creatures.

Read the following Scriptures and fill in the blanks.
Romans 8:17. God loves me enough to make me _____ with Christ.
2 Corinthians 3:18. God loves me enough to transform me into the _____ of Christ.
Ephesians 1:3. God loves me enough to bless me with _____.
1 John 3:1. God loves me enough to call me His _____.

God loves His own as fully and completely as any human could ever be loved by God—and His love knows no limits. That's what *eis telos* conveys.

But the expression *eis telos* also carries the idea of eternality. Here it speaks of a love that lasts forever. Not only did Christ love His own to the

Week of JULY 4

end of their lives; not only did He love them to the end of *His* earthly life; but He would love them eternally. In this same context, He tells them, "I go to prepare a place for you . . . that where I am, there you may be also" (14:2-3). His love for His own will be manifest throughout eternity.

So the phrase *eis telos* is rich with meaning: "Having loved His own who were in the world, He loved them *[eis telos]*"—to the uttermost in every respect.

Read John 15:13. What did Jesus say was the ultimate expression of love? _____
What did Jesus do one day after He made that statement? Read John 19:18. _____

This love of God for His own is not bestowed on people because they show themselves worthy of it. In fact, there is *nothing* worthy in the recipients of this love. Read Romans 5:6-8 in the margin. It is a wholly gracious love, not something anyone could ever earn through any kind of merit system.

Here is where the true greatness of divine love is seen. Christ faces the cross. He will bear their sin. And He will undergo the agonizing wrath of God on their behalf. He will suffer the painful, lonely sense of being forsaken by the Father, not to mention the human pain of execution and murder and public shame. And yet He is totally immersed in His love for His own, and as He faces death, He wants to affirm how much He loves these utterly unworthy ones.

"For while we were still helpless, at the right time Christ died for the ungodly. For one will hardly die for a righteous man; though perhaps for the good man someone would dare even to die. But God demonstrates His own love toward us, in that while we were yet sinners, Christ died for us" (Rom. 5:6-8, NASB).

This is a unique and marvelous love. It is a life-giving love. It is a love that pursues its object, no matter what. It is a love that saves forever. The particular love of God for His own is overwhelming. It is powerful. If you don't stand in awe of it, then you don't really grasp its significance. We ought to be in awe and humbled before such love. We have no right to God's love. He does not owe it to us. Yet He condescends to love us nonetheless. If our hearts aren't stirred with love for God in return, then there's something terribly wrong with us.

Read a portion of Jesus' prayer for His own in John 17:9-11,24-26. If you belong to Jesus, how does this prayer help you begin to sense the enormity of His love for you? _____

NOTES

To the Leader:

It's easy to get discouraged in the summer when class attendance and commitment seems to dip. Pray that your commitment level will remain high and that you will remain excited about Bible study. Continue to prepare for each lesson diligently regardless of whether you anticipate a full room or many empty chairs. The Holy Spirit doesn't require a classroom full of people to be active, just a willing, obedient heart.

Before the Session

1. Read *During the Session.* You probably won't have time to complete all the teaching steps. Choose the ones that best fit the needs and interest of your class.
2. If possible, do a commentary study of Matthew 22:1-14.

During the Session

1. Welcome participants. Open with prayer requests and prayer.
2. Invite the class to recite with you John 3:16 from memory. Ask: *What percentage of church-goers do you think can recite John 3:16 from memory? What percentage of church-goers do you think really understand what John 3:16 means? Explain.*
3. Ask someone to read John 3:16-18 from the Bible. Discuss how verses 17 and 18 are crucial to understanding God's love declared in verse 16.
4. Ask who God loves according to John 3:16. Inquire, *Does God love some people differently than He loves others?* Request that adults who respond to that question back up their responses with teachings from this week's study.
5. Invite someone to read Mark 10:17-23. Ask: *Do you think this young man really wanted to know how to obtain eternal life? If not, what do you think he wanted from Jesus? How have you observed people express an interest in Jesus for the same reasons? Has Jesus' answer to people's inquiries about eternal life changed over the centuries?* Request volunteers share their responses to the activity related to Mark 10:21-22 in Day 2. Ask each person to state the grade they gave the young man, then ask: *Are there really any in-between grades on how we respond to Jesus' call or is it a pass-fail test? How does God feel about those who fail the test?* (see verse 21). Explore this question: *If Jesus loved the man, why didn't He offer him eternal life at a cheaper price?*
6. Ask the class to name the four ways Dr. MacArthur stated God demonstrates love to all people. Write responses on the board. Ask someone to read Romans 3:10-18. Ask, *What is the only thing that*

Week of JULY 4

restrains the full wickedness of this human race? [Common grace] Request four volunteers read the Scripture passages in the first activity of Day 3 and lead the class to determine which evidence of common grace each passage proclaims. Discuss how each evidence of common grace is a sign of God's love for humanity.

7. Allow learners to tell what they think are the greatest things about being alive. Read aloud James 1:17. Ask, *How are the good things in life evidence of God's common grace?*
8. Ask someone to read the quotation in the margin in Day 3. Ask: *Does that statement comfort or discourage you? Why?*
9. Invite the class to follow along in their Bibles as you read Amos 4:6-12. Ask, *How does God express love through warnings such as this?*
10. Ask someone to read Jesus' parable in Matthew 22:1-14. Ask: *Who received the offer? Who ended up enjoying the banquet? Who experienced judgment?* Guide the class to make application of this parable to understand why some receive salvation while others do not.
11. Allow volunteers to share their responses to the last activity of Day 4.
12. Read John 13:1. Write *eis telos* on the board. Ask learners to recall from Day 5 how that term expresses the love God has for His own. Ask learners why they agree with Dr. MacArthur's statement, "If you don't stand in awe of God's love, then you don't really grasp its significance." Challenge learners to describe the lives of Christians who live in constant awareness of the love God has for them.
13. Allow a moment for silent prayer, encouraging learners to thank God for His marvelous love for them. Close in prayer, asking God that your class will spread the good news that He loved the world so much that He sent His Son.

After the Session

1. Read next week's lesson and complete the learning activities.
2. You may have several members out on vacation who missed this very important lesson. Consider sending an e-mail, explaining how this week's study challenged you to understand and appreciate God's love in new and different ways.

NOTES

Finding Security in the Love of God

George Matheson, a brilliant nineteenth-century Scottish pastor and hymn writer, was born with an eye defect that developed into total blindness by the time he was eighteen. Shortly thereafter, his fiancée left him, deciding she would not be content to be married to a blind man. And so it was in response to one of the gloomiest episodes of his life that Matheson penned his great hymn about the security of God's love, "O Love that Wilt Not Let Me Go." Spurned by what he thought was true love, he sought—and found—solace in the unchanging love of God:

> *O love that wilt not let me go,*
> *I rest my weary soul in thee.*
> *I give thee back the life I owe*
> *That in thine ocean-depths its flow*
> *May richer, fuller be.*

> "If God is on our side, it doesn't matter who is on the other side."
> —John MacArthur

The book of Romans is Paul's great treatise on justification by faith. In chapter 8, Paul declares that God's love is the supreme guarantee of the believer's security. He uses a succession of arguments, all based on the truth that salvation is solely God's work.

God Is for Us

"What then shall we say to these things? If *God is for us,* who is against us?" (v. 31, emphasis added). The argument is simple: If God is working to save us, nothing will thwart the work. Whatever God undertakes will most certainly be accomplished. And if God is on our side, it doesn't matter who is on the other side. God's side will be victorious. If God is for us, no one can stand against us.

Week of JULY 11

Someone has said that God plus one equals a majority. The truth is that God alone makes a majority. If every creature in the material and immaterial universe combined to oppose God together, still He would not be defeated. He is infinitely greater, and holier, and wiser, and more powerful than the aggregate of all His creation.

So the fact that He is working to save me makes the outcome certain. If my salvation were ultimately up to me, I would have much to fear. If my redemption hinged in any way on my abilities, I would be lost. Like any sinner, I'm prone to disobedience, unbelief, and weakness. If it were up to me alone to keep myself in the love of God, I would surely fail.

"The LORD is my light and my salvation; whom shall I fear? The LORD is the defense of my life; whom shall I dread?" (Ps. 27:1, NASB).

Read Psalm 27:1 and 46:1-2,11 in the margin. What recurring theme in these psalms echoes Paul's declaration that with God on our side, no one can stand against us?_____

"God is our refuge and strength, a very present help in trouble. Therefore we will not fear. . . . The LORD of hosts is with us; the God of Jacob is our stronghold" (Ps. 46:1-2,11, NASB).

The repeated refrain of Psalm 80 suggests that when the Lord causes His face to shine upon us, *"we will be saved"* (vv. 3,7,19, emphasis added). No doubt about it. When the Lord sets out to accomplish something, who can oppose Him?

If anyone could rob us of our salvation, that person would have to be greater than God Himself. God is for us. He has set His love on us. No human, no angel, not even Satan himself can alter that. So if God is for us, it matters not who is against us.

Yes, someone says, but can't Christians put themselves outside God's grace? What about those who commit abominable sins? Don't they nullify the work of redemption in themselves? Don't they forfeit the love of God?

Certainly not. That kind of thinking posits an impossible situation. Remember that we did not gain salvation by our own efforts, so it's preposterous to think that we can forfeit it by anything we do. We did not choose God in the first place; He chose us (John 15:16). We are drawn to Christ only by God's redeeming love (Jer. 31:3). His love continues to draw us and hold us. This is Paul's very point in Romans 8. God's love guarantees our security. That same love also guarantees our perseverance. "We love him, because he first loved us" (1 John 4:19, KJV). Now "the love of Christ controls us" (2 Cor. 5:14).

Read 1 Peter 1:3-5 and complete the following:

1. Record phrases that give evidence you can't earn your salvation. _____

2. Record phrases that give evidence you can't lose your salvation. _____

Thus, God's own love insures that we cannot do anything to remove ourselves from His grace.

We can no more forfeit the love of God than the prodigal son could destroy his father's love for him. Like the father of the prodigal son in Luke 15, God loves us constantly. He forgives eagerly, loves lavishly, and does not deal with us according to our sins, or reward us according to our iniquities (Ps. 103:10). Moreover, He does something the prodigal son's father could not do: He sovereignly draws us to Himself. His love is like a cord that draws us inexorably to Him (Hos. 11:4). "He chose us in [Christ] before the foundation of the world, that we should be holy and blameless before Him. In love He predestined us to adoption as sons through Jesus Christ to Himself, according to the kind intention of His will" (Eph. 1:4-5). And "whom He predestined . . . these He also glorified" (Rom. 8:30). God sees the process through to the end.

Our salvation is the work of God. God is "for us," and no one can deter Him from accomplishing what He has determined to do.

Revisit George Matheson's hymn and make it your own by completing the following:

O love that wilt not let me go—
   Describe times God's stubborn love has held on to you. _____

I rest my weary soul in thee—
   How has God's love given you rest? _____
_____

I give thee back the life I owe—
   How will you give your life to God today? _____
_____

Week of JULY 11

Christ Died for Us

Here's more proof that we are eternally secure: "He who did not spare His own Son, but *delivered Him up for us all*, how will He not also with Him freely give us all things?" (Rom. 8:32, emphasis added). God loves us regardless of the cost. Consider what God's love for us has already cost Him: He gave His own beloved Son to die in order to accomplish our salvation. Having already paid so great a price to redeem us, He won't allow the process to stop short of the goal. And if He has already given His best and dearest on our behalf, why would He withhold anything from us now?

Would God redeem sinners at the cost of His own Son's blood, then cast those same blood-bought believers aside? Having brought us to salvation at so great a price, would He then withhold any grace from us? Won't He finish what He started?

Read Philippians 1:6. Complete the statement below by writing a paraphrase of this promise:

I, God, personally guarantee to you that . . .

_____

Consider this: God gave Christ to die for us "while we were yet sinners" (Rom. 5:8). Would He turn His back on us now that we are justified? If He didn't spurn us when we were rebellious sinners, would He then cast us aside now that we are His children? "If while we were enemies, we were reconciled to God through the death of His Son" (Rom. 5:10), doesn't it seem reasonable that He will do everything necessary to keep us in the fold now that we are reconciled? If He gave us grace to trust Christ in the first place, He will assuredly give grace to keep us from falling away.

Psalm 84:11 says, "For the Lord God is a sun and shield: the Lord will give grace and glory: no good thing will he withhold from them that walk uprightly." God is not stingy with His grace, and the proof of that is seen in the sacrifice of Christ on our behalf.

> "... a faith and knowledge resting on the hope of eternal life, which God, who does not lie, promised before the beginning of time" (Titus 1:2, NIV).

The sacrifice of Christ is eternally bound up in God's love. Did you know that in eternity past, before God had even begun the work of creation, He promised to redeem? Titus 1:2 says the promise of eternal life was made "before the world began" (KJV)—literally, before the beginning of time. So this speaks of a divine promise made before anything was created.

Who made this promise and with whom was it made? Since it was made before creation commenced, there is only one possible answer: it was a promise made between the triune Members of the Godhead. God the Father, God the Son, and God the Spirit promised among themselves to redeem fallen humanity.

The plan of redemption was made not after Adam fell but before the beginning of creation. The saved are chosen in Christ "before the foundation of the world" (Eph. 1:4). God called us . . . in Christ Jesus from all eternity" (2 Tim. 1:9). The eternal kingdom is prepared for them "from the foundation of the world" (Matt. 25:34). Christ was foreordained to shed His blood on their behalf "before the foundation of the world" (1 Pet. 1:20). Their names are written in the Book of Life "from the foundation of the world" (Rev. 13:8; 17:8).

This means the plan of redemption is no contingency. It is not Plan B. It is no alternative strategy.

Furthermore, it means that the saved are God's gift of love to His Son. That's why Christ refers to them as "those whom Thou hast given Me" (John 17:9,24; 18:9). The Father has given them to Christ as a gift of love, and therefore not one of them will be lost. Both the Father and the Son work together to insure the fulfillment of their eternal plan of redemption. This further assures their salvation, for as Jesus said, "All that the Father gives Me shall come to Me, and the one who comes to Me I will certainly not cast out. . . . For this is the will of My Father, that everyone who beholds the Son and believes in Him, may have eternal life; and I Myself will raise him up on the last day" (John 6:37,40).

Have you ever considered yourself God's gift to His Son? ❏ Yes ❏ No

How does that fact make you feel? (Circle all that apply)

Skeptical   Unbelievably loved   Valuable   Secure

Other? _____

Week of JULY 11

So Christ Himself promises to see God's plan of redemption through to the end. Having died as a substitute for those whom the Father gave Him, He promises to see the process through to the final consummation in glory. Likewise, the Father, having already given His Son to die on our behalf, will not now withhold anything necessary to complete our redemption.

God Himself Justifies Us

Remember that the theme of Paul's epistle to the Romans is justification by faith. Paul began chapter 8 with a crucial statement about justification.

Read Romans 8:1. Write the verse here.

_____

_____

There is a wealth of theology in that verse. It draws together all the threads of truth about justification that the apostle had been weaving in the preceding chapters.

Paul had been teaching the Romans that justification is a forensic event whereby God forgives the sins of those who believe and imputes to them a perfect righteousness. In chapter 4, for example, he spoke of believers as "Those whose lawless deeds have been forgiven, and whose sins have been covered" (v. 7). The Lord does not take their sins into account (v. 8). And what's more, righteousness is reckoned to their account (v. 11). Therefore, they stand before God without fear of His righteous judgment (8:1).

All this hinges on the fact that they are "in Christ."

Read Romans 6:3-5. What are the key words in this passage that help you understand what it means to be "in Christ"? _____

_____

So consider the implications of this doctrine: Those who are "in Christ" have their sins completely forgiven; they have all the merit of Christ Himself imputed to their account. God Himself has undertaken to justify them. Christ has accomplished redemption on their behalf. They stand in God's favor solely because He decided to show grace to them, not because of anything they did to earn it. Therefore, Paul asks, if God declares them not guilty, who is going to condemn them? "Who will bring a charge against God's elect? *God is the one who justifies;* who is the one who condemns? (8:33-34, emphasis added).

There's a tremendous amount of security in the doctrine of justification by faith. It is because of this doctrine that we can rest in our salvation as an accomplished fact. Jesus said, "Truly, truly, I say to you, he who hears My word, and believes Him who sent Me, has eternal life, and does not come into judgment, but has passed out of death into life" (John 5:24). As Paul says, "There is therefore now no condemnation for those who are in Christ Jesus" (Rom. 8:1). It's a done deal, not a goal we work toward. Eternal life is a present possession, not a future hope. And our justification is a declaration that takes place in the court of heaven, so no earthly judge can alter the verdict. When God Himself says "not guilty," who can say otherwise?

Check the statement that best describes you:
❑ **I am my own worst critic and condemn myself regularly.**
❑ **I feel so condemned by other people.**
❑ **I live secure in the knowledge that I am not condemned because God says so.**

What will you do today to begin making the last statement a reality in your life? _____

Our Heavenly High Priest Intercedes for Us

The ongoing work of Christ is yet another reason we cannot fall out of favor with God.

Week of JULY 11

Read Romans 8:34.
What work does Christ continually do on our behalf?
_____

Read Hebrews 7:25.
What does Christ accomplish in the lives of those for whom He intercedes? _____
_____

Jesus' ongoing intercession on our behalf guarantees our salvation "forever"—literally, to the uttermost.

Read Romans 8:26.
How does Christ pray for you? _____
_____

Surely what Jesus prays is similar to the great high priestly prayer recorded in John 17.

State what Jesus prays for you in the following verses from John 17.
Verses 11-12: _____
Verses 14-15: _____
Verse 17: _____
Verses 21-23: _____

In short, He is praying that we will be kept in the faith, that we might "never perish," and that no one would snatch us out of His hand (John 10:28).

Will that prayer be answered? Certainly. In fact, to deny that the believer is secure in Christ and secure in the love of God, is to deny that Christ's priestly work is sufficient. And to doubt whether the believer might fall out of favor with God is to misunderstand God's love for His own.

"Christ Jesus is He who died, yes, rather who was raised, who is at the right hand of God, who also intercedes for us" (Rom. 8:34, NASB).

"He is able to save forever those who draw near to God through Him, since He always lives to make intercession for them" (Heb. 7:25, NASB).

"In the same way the Spirit also helps our weakness; for we do not know how to pray as we should, but the Spirit Himself intercedes for us with groanings too deep for words" (Rom. 8:26, NASB).

John MacARTHUR, JR.

Nothing Can Separate Us from the Love of God in Christ Jesus

Paul wraps up his discourse on the believer's security in Romans 8 in verses 35-39. These closing verses read like a hymn on the love of God.

Read those verses now.
What is the first question Paul asked? _____
In one word, give Paul's answer to his question. ____

"In all these things we overwhelmingly conquer through Him who loved us" (v. 37). It's a no-lose situation—because of the love of God.

The various threats Paul outlined were not hypothetical dilemmas as far as he was concerned.

In the margin, list the hardships noted in Romans 8:35.

Paul had faced those very hardships—and others as well.

As you read 2 Corinthians 11:23-27, draw a checkmark next to the trials listed in the margin that Paul personally experienced. Draw a star next to those trials you have faced.

Paul emerged from his trials with an unshaken confidence in the love of God. Have you? ❑ Yes ❑ No

In Romans 8:36 Paul quotes Psalm 44:22 by way of reminder that the people of God have always suffered: "For Thy sake we are killed all day long; we are considered as sheep to be slaughtered." God's love does not necessarily guarantee earthly comfort. But the sufferings of this world are more than compensated by the rewards of divine love in eternal bliss. As Paul wrote earlier in Romans 8, "I consider that the sufferings of this present time are not worthy to be compared with the glory that is to be revealed to us" (v. 18; see also 2 Cor. 4:17).

> "Ultimately the love of God is the basis for all our hopes."
> —John MacArthur

Week of JULY 11

"The glory that is to be revealed to us" is God's glory. The general love God has toward all humanity reveals His basic goodness. The fact that it is spurned by those who do not believe in no way diminishes God's glory. Even the wrath of sinful men shall praise Him (Ps. 76:10). But the riches of His goodness and glory are revealed most clearly in the salvation of sinners, a great multitude that no man could ever number (Rev. 7:9).

Why is all this so important? Ultimately the love of God is the basis for all our hopes. It is the object of our deepest longings. It is the source and fulfillment of our faith. It is the very basis for His grace to us. After all, we love Him only because He first loved us (1 John 4:19). His love is also our guarantee of eternal bliss. Since He loved us enough to send His own Son to die for us while we were yet His enemies—we have no reason to fear losing that love, now that His Spirit has been sent forth into our hearts, enabling us to cry, "Abba, Father!" (Gal. 4:5). His love absolutely permeates and envelops every aspect of our lives in Christ.

As Christians, then, we ought to see that everything we enjoy in life—from our tiniest pleasures to the eternal redemption we have found in Christ—is an expression of the great love wherewith God loved us (Eph. 2:4). The blessing of His love comes to us not because we deserve it, but simply and only because of His grace. For certainly we do not deserve His blessing, but the very opposite. Yet He pours out His love without measure, and we are invited to partake of its benefits freely.

What is your response to that kind of love?

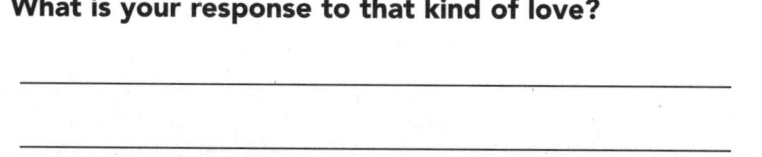

If you have enjoyed these Bible studies from John MacArthur and desire to purchase your own copy of his book The God Who Loves to read and study in greater detail, visit the LifeWay Christian Store serving you. Or, you can order a copy by calling 1-800-233-1123.

As recipients of love like that, we can only fall on our faces in wonder. When we contemplate such love, it ought to make us feel unworthy. Yet at the same time it lifts us to unimaginable heights of joy and confidence, because we know that our God, the righteous judge of all the universe, the One to whom we have by faith committed our very souls' well-being—has revealed Himself as a God of immeasurable love. And we are the objects of that love—despite our unworthiness and despite our sin! In light of the glories of divine love, how can we not be utterly lost in wonder, love, and praise?

NOTES

To the Leader:

Read Romans 8 every day this week. How does it comfort you? How does it challenge you? How will you internalize this portion of God's Word so that your very life teaches the lesson of security in the love of God?

Before the Session

1. Read *During the Session.* Choose the teaching steps you will use.
2. Enlist volunteers to be prepared to read John 15:16; Ephesians 1:4; and Jeremiah 31:3.

During the Session

1. Welcome participants. Open with prayer requests and prayer.
2. Ask: *What kinds of guarantees are offered to entice us to buy a product? For what kind of items do you insist on a guarantee before you purchase? Why? How do guarantees give us a sense of security? What did Dr. MacArthur declare is the supreme guarantee of a believer's eternal security?*
3. Draw a line down the board to create two columns. In one column write the name or initials of each learner present. (If you have a large class just write "Our Class.") Encourage participants to name problems common to adults today. Write responses in the second column. Read Romans 8:31 aloud and ask, *What does Roman 8:31 say about these problems we face?* Request someone read the quotation in the margin of Day 1. Draw an X through the second column. Write "God" over the names in the first column and state: *Who we are isn't really an issue either! It's all about God.*
4. To help the class explore God's role in salvation, ask volunteers to share their response to question 1 from the 1 Peter activity in Day 1. Ask the pre-enlisted volunteers to read John 15:16; Ephesians 1:4; and Jeremiah 31:3 and direct participants to state how God's mercy is displayed in those passages. To explore how God continues to guarantee our salvation, ask for responses to question 2 of the 1 Peter activity. Request participants silently read 1 Peter 1:3-5 and state the actions God takes. Then ask them to state the actions the believer takes. Point out the believer does nothing except praise God!
5. Read aloud Romans 8:31-32. Ask, *If God has paid such a great price to save us, what can we depend on Him to do?* Allow volunteers to share their paraphrase of Philippians 1:6. Ask, *At what times of your life do you especially need to be reminded of that promise?*

Week of JULY 11

6. Request a volunteer read Romans 5:6-11. Ask participants to share truths from this passage that just don't seem logical. [Christ died for us when we were His enemies.] Then ask them to state the logical conclusion of this passage. Guide the class to understand that if Christ died for them when they were His enemies, it's only logical He would preserve their salvation once they are His beloved children.
7. Read aloud Romans 7:18-24. Ask if participants can name the person who wrote those words. [The apostle Paul.] Ask: *What conclusion did Paul draw about his natural self? Does it surprise you to hear the great apostle make such a statement? Why?* Ask someone to read what Paul wrote just two verses later in Romans 8:1. Inquire: *Now what conclusion does Paul make about himself? How did he make such a drastic jump from being wretched to being justified?* Lead the class to identify the phrase in Romans 8:1 on which justification is based. To explore the meaning of "in Christ," request volunteers share their responses to the Romans 6 activity in Day 3.
8. Ask: *What percentage of Christians live like they believe the truth of Romans 8:31? How can we live like people who are free from condemnation?*
9. Ask someone to read Romans 8:34 and ask the class to state another reason they can be secure in their salvation. Invite someone to read Romans 8:26 and ask, *What freedom do you find in this verse?* [Even praying the right words isn't up to you!] Ask adults to state what Jesus prays for His followers.
10. Ask participants to state whether they think the word *stubborn* is a positive or negative term and to state why. Direct them to listen for evidences of God's stubborn love as you read aloud Romans 8:35-39. Call for responses.
11. Read Dr. MacArthur's statement, "Ultimately the love of God is the basis for all our hopes." Allow volunteers to share how God's stubborn love for them has been the basis for their hope, joy, and peace.
12. Close in prayer.

NOTES

After the Session

1. Read next week's lesson and complete the learning activities.
2. Contact absentees and let them know they were missed.

ABOUT THE WRITERS

Josh McDowell and Bob Hostetler

Dr. McDowell is an internationally known speaker, author, and traveling representative for Campus Crusade for Christ. He has authored or coauthored more than 60 books, including *More Than a Carpenter* and *The New Evidence That Demands a Verdict*. He and his wife live in Dallas, Texas.

Bob Hostetler is an award-winning writer, editor, pastor, and speaker. Bob and his family live in Oxford, Ohio.

AMY SUMMERS wrote the personal learning activities and teaching plans this quarter. Amy is an experienced writer for LifeWay Bible study curriculum, a mother, and a Sunday School leader from Arden, North Carolina. She is a graduate of Baylor University and Southwestern Baptist Theological Seminary.

ABOUT THIS STUDY

Identify "the three pillars" in the following Scriptures:

John 1:14 _____

Acts 10:39-41 _____

Acts 13:26-34 _____

Romans 1:1-4 _____

1 Corinthians 15:3-7 _____

Colossians 1:15-20 _____

Hebrews 4:12 _____

2 Peter 1:20-21 _____

Beyond Belief to Convictions

As an adult Christian studying these lessons, you may find you haven't fully come to understand why you believe what you believe. I find that many Christian adults haven't carefully examined how Christ and His Word are objectively true and relationally meaningful to the point of being able to explain it to others. But if we adults are going to guide our kids into deepened Christian convictions, we must have deepened Christian convictions too. In fact, you may even find you have unwittingly adopted some of the postmodern mind-set that the younger generation has adopted. In many respects, these lessons will first equip you—the Christian adult reader—with renewed convictions in Christ and His Word so you can pass on your faith effectively to the next generation.

Throughout these lessons we will explore what I call *the three fundamental pillars of Christianity*:

- Christ's deity and incarnation
- The reliability of Scripture
- The resurrection of Christ.

I trust that as we look at these pillars together, you will capture a renewed vision of who Christ is and why He came to earth; understand how reliable God's Word is and why He so carefully preserved it for you; and be challenged with an optimistic perspective on life and your future as we explore the reality of Christ's death and resurrection. As we examine each of these pillars together, we will encounter not only the objective truth of these things but also see how they are relationally meaningful to our lives—a meaning that answers the very fundamental questions of our lives.

Josh McDowell

Josh MCDOWELL

A Crisis of Belief

day One

As the three Christian leaders gathered before dawn in a place they thought to be secret, their prayer time together was interrupted by a cadre of Roman soldiers. They were lifted to their feet, shackled, and led away to an unknown destination.

After several anxious hours of imprisonment, the Christians were brought out before a raucous crowd in the arena of the Colosseum. Still in chains, the group stood before the proconsul, who ordered them, "Renounce your false beliefs, and I will release you." He added a warning: "Fail to swear the oath, and you will face the lions."

All three affirmed their faith in Christ. The proconsul hesitated only a moment before lifting his hand with a flourish. "Then you have made your choice," he said. He nodded, and the soldiers opened the gates. The crowd erupted in a bloodthirsty frenzy as the lions appeared in the arena and focused their hungry gazes on their prey.

> **Read Hebrews 11:37-38. In the margin, list the types of persecutions early believers endured.**
> **What did God say about believers who chose persecution rather than renounce their faith?**

_____

Dangers in a Twenty-First-Century Colosseum

In many ways, our young people today must endure a twenty-first-century Colosseum. They may not face literal lions, but they quite possibly encounter more ethical and moral temptations, greater spiritual battles and more intense emotional and relational struggles than any other generation in history. I know that your prayer—like mine—is that our kids

Sidebar: "They were stoned, they were sawed in two, they died by the sword, they wandered about in sheepskins, in goatskins, destitute, afflicted, and mistreated. The world was not worthy of them. They wandered in deserts, mountains, caves, and holes in the ground" (Heb. 11:37-38, HCSB).

Week of JULY 18

will be strong in spirit and character, able to resist the pressures of a godless culture.

But we worry that the values we are trying to instill within our children will be countered somehow. What strikes fear in our hearts is the possibility that our young people will fall prey to the wrong crowd, succumb to the cultural pressures, and make wrong choices that will bring pain and suffering to their lives. We're concerned that all the warnings, cautions, and biblical teachings we offer our children won't be enough to ground them and keep them standing strong. We have ample reason for alarm.

Read 1 Peter 5:8-9. How does the Bible identify the "lion" believers face? _____

What does this "lion" desire to do with our young people (and all people)? _____

How firm is the faith in which you stand?
❑ I have no faith.
❑ My faith has the consistency of a congealed salad.
❑ My faith shifts like sand on the beach.
❑ My faith is rock-solid.

"Be sober! Be on the alert! Your adversary the Devil is prowling around like a roaring lion, looking for anyone he can devour. Resist him, firm in the faith, knowing that the same sufferings are being experienced by your brothers in the world" (1 Pet. 5:8-9, HCSB).

Why Beliefs Matter

While we need to fear what our kids could be tempted to *do,* we need to be more concerned with what our kids are led to *believe.* You see, the way our kids behave comes *from* something. Their attitudes and actions spring from their value system, and their value system is based on what they believe.

It is my belief that the three fundamental pillars of Christianity—Christ's deity and incarnation, the reliability of Scripture, and the resurrection of Christ—correspond directly to and are relationally meaningful to the three fundamental questions of our lives—Who am I? Why am I here? and Where am I going?

"WHO AM I?" AND THE PERSON OF JESUS

In varying degrees, all of us sometimes feel adrift, alone, and alienated from others. Many experts believe such feelings are epidemic and severe among today's youth. Most of our kids are not sure who they are, who they belong to, or where they fit in. Even kids who have the benefit of a relatively functional family still at times wonder, *Who am I?* Indeed, we all want to know somehow that we are of value. We want to know we are loved and accepted. Each of us is silently asking, *Who am I?* But few are finding a satisfying answer.

Astonishingly, the answer to that question is also the key that will correct our kids' distorted beliefs about God. The truth about Jesus Christ—that He is God who became flesh and lived among us—can unlock the secret to our identity. The overwhelming evidence of Christ's deity is not only sufficient to convince our minds that it is objectively true but also amazingly meaningful to each of us individually because it enables us to discover our true identity. Thus, understanding this truth will change the way we view God and ourselves.

Look up and read Galatians 4:4-7 and 1 John 4:9-10. How would you use the truth of Christ's incarnation declared in these verses to answer a person's question, "Who am I?" _____

"WHY AM I HERE?" AND THE WORD OF GOD

Our children and young people also are searching for the answer to the question, *Why am I here?*

When we and our kids examine the abundance of evidence for the Bible's reliability and the extraordinary means by which the Bible has been preserved, our minds and hearts will be convinced that the biblical record is an accurate and true reflection of the God who desires a relationship with us. And when we understand what that reliable Word means to our lives, we will discover our God-given purpose in life. Exploring that truth and its meaning will convince us and enable us to urge our kids beyond belief to conviction.

"WHERE AM I GOING?" AND THE RESURRECTION OF CHRIST

It doesn't take long for any of us, including our young people, to realize that life is full of disappointments. That's an unavoidable conclusion.

Week of JULY 18

Tragedies like the Oklahoma City bombing, the Columbine shootings, and the terrorist attacks in America emotionally reinforce that we live in an uncertain world. But how we and our kids handle the disappointments and heartaches in life is critical. Far too often our tragedies and disappointments in life turn to despondency and despair. We may even become resentful and angry about what has happened. In the highly competitive and cruel world of today's youth culture, the optimism of a pre-teen turns to pessimism in the teen years.

At such times, one fundamental question becomes even more pressing: *Where am I going?* And neither our kids' distorted beliefs about reality nor the mind-set that dominates today's culture can satisfactorily answer that question for our kids. But there is an answer, and it, too, is tied into one of the three pillars of Christianity.

When we and our kids are led to examine the evidences for the resurrection of Christ, we discover the objective truth of that historical event. But more than that, we also discover that the resurrection of Christ is profoundly meaningful in times of disappointment and disaster. In fact, convictions about the truth and meaning of the Resurrection can actually change our entire outlook on life and provide us with such a sense of destiny that we and our kids can face life or death, good or evil, triumph or tragedy with a spirit of gratitude, optimism, and courage.

Look up and read Romans 8:34-35 and 1 Peter 1:3-5. In the margin list all the results of Christ's resurrection that empower you personally to face life courageously and optimistically.

Distorted Beliefs

What may surprise you is that the majority of our young people don't even hold to a biblical belief system. Our kids, even those from solid Christian homes and churches, have distorted beliefs about God and the Bible that are having a devastating rippling affect into every aspect of their lives.

Since beliefs shape values, and values lead to exhibit specific attitudes and actions, this is precisely why studies reveal that young people who lack a basic biblical belief system are:
- 225 percent more likely to be angry with life
- 216 percent more likely to be resentful
- 210 percent more likely to lack purpose in life
- 200 percent more likely to be disappointed in life

But beliefs create values that result not only in certain attitudes but also in specific behaviors. That's why research also has shown that otherwise good kids from good families who don't possess a biblical belief system are:
- 36 percent more likely to lie to a friend
- 48 percent more likely to cheat on an exam
- 200 percent more likely to steal
- 200 percent more likely to physically hurt someone
- 300 percent more likely to use illegal drugs
- 600 percent more likely to attempt suicide

While this may be disturbing, it should not surprise us, because our actions flow out of our values, which arise from our beliefs.

> "A good man produces good things from his storeroom of good, and an evil man produces evil things from his storeroom of evil" (Matt. 12:35, HCSB).

Read Matthew 12:35. Create a flow chart in the margin using the information in the previous paragraphs that illustrates the principle in this passage.

OUR KIDS' DISTORTED BELIEFS

I realize that many parents and gatekeepers will tell me they have good kids and they're so impressed with the attitudes of their young people. And, in part, research bears this out.
- 65 percent of today's young people want a close relationship with God
- 49 percent want to make a difference in the world
- 79 percent consider having close personal friends as a high priority goal for their future

Based on the research, if I had to summarize in one sentence what I believe kids want, I would say *they want a healthy, relationally significant life on earth and a home in heaven.* Today's young people appear to be the most occupationally and educationally ambitious generation ever, and they possess a high degree of spiritual interest. Indeed, four out of five teens (80 percent) say their religious beliefs are very important in their lives.

Week of JULY 18

But because you and I care about the future of our young people, we must look at what our kids are really believing in three areas—their beliefs about God, truth, and reality. For it is what our kids believe that will eventually define everything they come to be, as well as determine the most important choices they make in life. And what our kids currently believe is alarming.

1. Our Kids Are Adopting Distorted Beliefs about God.

Gather a group of teenagers together—good Christian kids—and ask them, "Who do you think God is?" "What do you think God is like?" How do you think they would respond? _____

_____

This generation may be open and vocal about their faith—even to the point of wearing their Christian witness on T-shirts and WWJD bracelets—but many of them are defining God in their own ways. While the vast majority of our teens (80 percent) believe that God created the universe, and 84 percent believe that God is personally involved in people's lives, 63 percent also believe that Muslims, Buddhists, Christians, Jews, and all other people pray to the same god, even though they use different names for their god.

And what did these teens say they believe about Jesus?

Your child or youth group may believe that Jesus really lived and that He was actually born of a virgin. Your son or daughter may even be among the minority who believe Christ rose from the dead. But the vast majority of our own kids (65 percent) either believes or suspects that there is no way to tell which religion is true! Their view of God is so distorted that they're not convinced the Jesus of the Bible is the way, the truth, and the life for "all the children of the world."

2. Our Kids Are Embracing Distorted Beliefs about Truth.

How our young people determine what is true (and what is good) is alarming. Today's culture encourages young people to "figure it out" themselves, and what most are "figuring out" is a little truth here and a little error there until they end up with erroneous beliefs.

"Jesus told him, 'I am the way, the truth, and the life. No one comes to the Father except through Me'" (John 14:6, HCSB).

On the vertical line below, indicate how strongly you believe Jesus' assertion about Himself by placing a mark where you would locate yourself.

"Don't believe at all"

|
|
|
|

"Believe completely"

The importance of two tiny words—*to me*—must not be underestimated. Our young people today are not looking to the biblical text for moral truth. In fact, the majority of today's youth (70 percent) say there is no absolute moral truth. They are actually looking within themselves for moral truth. Young people simply hear truth through their own "filter," which tells them that all truth is subjectively and personally determined. Today's young people have been conditioned to believe that truth is not true for them *until they choose to believe it*. That's why 81 percent of our kids claim that "all truth is relative to the individual and his/her circumstances."

3. Our Kids Are Accepting Distorted Beliefs about Reality.
Today's young people have also become very pragmatic; they want what is real, relevant, and "right now."

Seventy two percent of our teens believe that "you can tell if something is morally/ethically right for you by whether or not it works in your life." Consequently, our kids feel no need to discuss such abstract ideas as the absolute truth of God's Word; they see little reason to grapple with what they believe about Christ and why. "What's the point?" they say, "as long as it works for me, that's all I care about." Thus, they see no big difference between what seems to work for the moment and what is right.

If you desire to dig deeper . . .

Read the following verses and record what you discover about truth:
- Zechariah 8:19
- John 1:17
- John 8:31-32
- John 17:17
- 2 Timothy 4:3-4

Circle the word(s) that best describe your thoughts after today's study.

| Discouraged | Disturbed | Determined |
| Depressed | Disagree | Other: |

Postmodernism and Its Effects

Who's teaching kids these distorted things? And how are they doing it without my knowledge? The culprit in this case is not a person but a philosophy that permeates much of our culture—government, schools, movies, television, and music. It is a widespread cultural mind-set and influence known as *postmodernism*.

Week of JULY 18

Trying to define and truly understand postmodernism can be a lot like standing in an appliance store trying to watch three or four television shows at once. Postmodernism defies definition because it is extremely complex, often contradictory, and constantly changing. Postmodernism repudiates any appeal to reality or truth. So, while postmodernism is tough to pin down, it is possible to summarize its most common beliefs:

• Truth does not exist in any objective sense. Instead of "discovering" truth in a meta-narrative—which is a story (such as the Bible) or ideology (such as Marxism) that presents a unified way of looking at philosophy, religion, art, and science—postmodernism rejects any overarching explanation of what constitutes truth and reality.

• Truth—whether in science, education, or religion—is created by a specific culture or community and is "true" only in and for that culture.

• Individual persons are the product of their cultures. That is, we are not essentially unique individuals created in the image of God; our identities are defined by our culture (African-American, European, Eastern, Western, urban, rural, and so forth).

• All thinking is a "social construct." In other words, what you and I regard as "truths" are simply arbitrary beliefs we have been conditioned to accept by our society, just as others have been conditioned to accept a completely different set of beliefs.

• Any system or statement that claims to be objectively true or unfavorably judges the values, beliefs, lifestyles, and truth claims of another culture is a power play, an effort by one culture to dominate other cultures.

Let's take a minute to review. To the best of your understanding, what is truth as defined by postmodernism? _____

Our young people have embraced these concepts, and they've done it, more or less, while we were napping. As a result, we have been slow to understand postmodernism's impact and counter its influence. And because most of our kids seem to have a keen interest in spiritual things, most adults are not alarmed. But as I said before, we have reason for alarm. As the studies show, the postmodern influence has had a profound effect on what our kids believe about God, truth, and reality.

Thus, while young people may be willing to believe that Christianity offers *a* "truth," they're not convinced it is *the* truth, the only hope for salvation and relationship with the God of the universe. Also, they are not trying to understand the objective truth of God's Word and live out that truth in their lives. Therefore, our kids are using Scripture merely as a springboard for thought as they attempt to create their own personal "meaning," one that may have little or nothing to do with the objective meaning of the biblical text.

Consequently, our young people have bought into a line of reasoning that says, "Don't bore me with your rules, your values, or your belief systems. And don't tell me what to think. I'm supposed to figure out what works myself, in the real world."

> "But if I should be delayed, I have written so that you will know how people ought to act in God's household, which is the church of the living God, the pillar and foundation of the truth"
> (1 Tim. 3:15, HCSB).

> "The Lord's slave must not quarrel, but must be gentle to everyone, able to teach, and patient, instructing his opponents with gentleness. Perhaps God will grant them repentance to know the truth. Then they may come to their senses and escape the Devil's trap, having been captured by him to do his will"
> (2 Tim. 2:24-26, HCSB).

Read 1 Timothy 3:15 and 2 Timothy 2:24-26. What is the responsibility of the church in combating this distorted belief about reality? _____

Time Is Running Out

It *does matter* what our kids believe about God and His Word. Their ability to stand strong morally, spiritually, emotionally, and relationally is at stake. The time is now for every denomination, parachurch ministry, local church, and family to ground their children and young people in what we believe as Christians and why we believe it. This is important not just because our kids need to adopt our values but also because their very understanding of the meaning of life depends on it.

In the lessons that follow we will explain how deepened beliefs in God and His Word can so ground a person in his or her relationship with God that he or she will answer the fundamental questions of life: "Who am I?" "Why am I here?" "Where am I going?" Leading our young people to truly know the one true God will help our kids find their true sense of identity, purpose, and destiny in life. Then they will be fortified spiritually, morally, and emotionally to stand strong in the face of today's culture.

But we must not delay. Time is running out. Let me put it this way. I have often said, "The youth of today will be the church of tomorrow."

Week of JULY 18

But I'm afraid I can't say that anymore because if we don't do something *now* to reeducate our kids in the foundations of the Christian faith, the young people we're counting on to lead the church into the next generation won't even *be in* the church of the next generation!

I realize I haven't painted a very pretty picture. Yet I believe there is still hope. I am hopeful, first, because although our kids do have distorted beliefs about God, truth, and reality, few of them have solidified their positions. The studies reveal that 74 percent of our kids are still trying to figure out the purpose and meaning of their lives, and 63 percent admit they don't have any set philosophy about life that consistently influences their lifestyles and decisions. That gives us a wide-open window of opportunity to counter their distorted views and clarify with them what they should believe—and why.

Second, I'm hopeful because there *is* an effective way to counter the cultural conditioning that has distorted our kids' belief systems. I know of no better way to reverse the effect of a postmodern worldview than to bring our kids face-to-face with true biblical Christianity. True Christianity not only effectively counters subjective believing, the loss of moral absolutes, and distorted perceptions of reality, it can also transform a person's behavior so that he or she will no longer be "tossed here and there by waves, and carried about by every wind of doctrine" (Ephesians 4:14, NASB).

I believe that is what you and I want for our young people. We want them to stand strong. We want them to be twenty-first-century expressions of Christ's body, living as "children of God without fault in a crooked and depraved generation, in which [they] shine like stars in the universe" (Philippians 2:15, NIV). But in order for that to happen, we must first help them identify their distorted beliefs and move them beyond their subjective belief systems to a set of solid convictions in the one true God. Then we can help them develop an objective faith in God as real, relevant, and right now.

> **Draw several stars below. In the stars, write the names of young people you desire to see shine like stars in the universe. Ask God to show you how He wants you to be involved in presenting truth to these young people. Commit to pray for them daily, perhaps using the Scriptures listed in the margin as a guide for your prayers.**

Proverbs 3:1-4
Proverbs 4:1-27
Proverbs 23:15-25
2 Timothy 2:22

Amy SUMMERS

leader Guide

NOTES

To the Leader:

Remember that teaching plans are simply a guide, not an exact blueprint to follow.

Choose teaching activities and personal learning activities from the daily studies that best fit the personality and needs of your group.

Prepare each lesson carefully, asking the Father to help you "correctly handle the word of truth" (2 Timothy 2:15, NIV).

Before the Session

1. Secure three 16-ounce plastic cups. On one side of each cup write one of the three pillars of Christianity.
2. Provide index cards for each learner present.
3. Study and meditate on the Scriptures in the interactive learning activity under "About This Study" on page 82.

During the Session

1. Welcome participants. Open with prayer requests and prayer.
2. Display the three plastic cups. (Face the words on each cup towards you.) Ask the class to imagine the cups are pillars. Ask: *What is their purpose as pillars? What did Dr. McDowell identify as the three fundamental pillars of Christianity?* As participants name each pillar, turn the corresponding cup around so the words are visible to the class.
3. Request volunteers look up the Scripture references in the interactive learning activity under "About This Study" on page 82 and read the passages aloud. Lead the class to identify the pillar(s) presented in each passage. Ask, *Why do you think these three particular theological truths are fundamental pillars of our Christian faith?*
4. Distribute index cards to each participant. Instruct learners to review the last paragraph of the Study Theme Introduction and state what Dr. McDowell desires to happen in each person as your class examines these three pillars. Instruct participants to write each desired result on their index card. Encourage learners to keep this card in their Bibles and consult it periodically throughout the study to determine if they are beginning to gain a renewed vision of who Christ is and why He came to earth, the reliability and purpose of God's Word, and the reality of Christ's death and resurrection.
5. Arrange the three plastic cups in a triangle and place your index card on top on them. Ask, *What will happen to my belief system if one of these pillars is removed?* Remove one of the cups so your card falls off. (You may need to practice this so you can be certain your card

Week of JULY 18

actually does fall!) State, *We must base our faith on all three pillars; we can't pick and choose what we want to believe.* Lead the class to determine how all three pillars are interconnected. Ask a volunteer to read 1 Corinthians 15:12-20. Explore that passage's relevance to your discussion.

6. Ask why it is imperative for Christian adults to stand firm in their beliefs. Discuss how this study can be relevant to all participants, even those who aren't parents or whose children are grown.
7. Ask participants why they agreed or disagreed with Dr. McDowell's statement in the first paragraph under Day 2 on page 85.
8. As volunteers read Galatians 4:4-7 and 1 John 4:9-10, direct the class to listen for evidences of Christ's incarnation. Ask, *How does the deity and incarnation of Jesus give us an identity and confirm our value?*
9. Ask volunteers to read Romans 6:4-11 and Acts 2:24. Ask, *How can the truth of the Resurrection found in these verses change a person's outlook toward life and death and provide a sense of destiny?* You may choose to continue your discussion of the Resurrection by allowing volunteers to share their responses to the last activity of Day 2.
10. Request half the class silently read Isaiah 59:9-15 and the other half read Jeremiah 9:3-6. Instruct learners to note similarities between the people in Scripture and today's generation described in Day 3. After a few moments, allow volunteers to share. Ask, *What is our responsibility as Christian adults to this generation that doesn't believe in absolute truth?* (Refer them to the final activity in Day 4.) Lead adults to identify specific ways your church can be a pillar and foundation of truth in your community.
11. As a closing prayer, encourage each participant to look up one of the passages in the margin of Day 5. Encourage learners to voice a portion of these Scriptures (silently or out loud) as a prayer for the youth in your church.

After the Session

1. Read next week's lesson and complete the learning activities.
2. If any participant expressed doubt in the absolute truths you studied today, schedule a time to meet and discuss this further.

NOTES

From Beliefs to Convictions

day One

Why "Believing" Is Not Enough

In centuries past, young men and women found the strength to stand up for what they believed, even in the face of pressure and persecution.

> **Read Acts 4:13-20. Circle the word(s) that describe Peter and John's response to pressure.**
> **Defiant   Courageous   Rebellious   Faithful**
> **Determined   Angry   Other** _____

"So what do we have to do," you might ask, "to equip our children and young people to resist the pressures of a godless culture and stand up for what they believe? Do we simply teach them to believe the right things? Is that the answer?"

That may seem logical, but it's not that simple. Getting our kids to believe in the right things won't be enough. Your children and mine live in a culture that is radically different from the one you and I experienced in our formative years. Theirs is more like the culture the early Christians faced two thousand years ago. Today's culture is completely intolerant of anyone who believes in absolute truth—that is, a truth that exists outside ourselves, one that is true for all people, for all times, for all places. Consequently, if our young people assert—or even suggest—that what they believe is absolutely and equally true for everyone, they will face widespread scorn and quite possibly persecution.

> **Read Galatians 4:16. What do the apostle Paul and young believers today have in common?** _____
>
> _____

Week of JULY 25

Thus, if our kids are going to hold firmly to their faith in such circumstances, it is not enough for them to "just believe" or give mere intellectual assent to certain things about God and the Bible, *even* if those beliefs are correct doctrine. Because of the pressures they face and the influences they reflect, our kids will require something *beyond belief.* In short, we must help them move beyond belief to *convictions.*

Developing Convictions about What We Believe

To *believe* in something is to "accept it as true, genuine or real." To the majority of this generation, including our own kids, nothing is objectively true, universally genuine, or actually real in an absolute sense. That is why we must help move our kids beyond a personal, subjective belief to belief with convictions.

To have *convictions* is to be thoroughly convinced that something is true. A conviction goes beyond having a personal preference about something. It goes deeper than a subjective opinion. Having convictions is being so thoroughly convinced that something is absolutely true that you take a stand for it regardless of the consequences. That's the kind of belief in God and his Word our kids need.

That's the kind of belief Daniel had. He was unwilling to compromise his beliefs and practices even though it meant facing a den of ravenous lions. That same kind of committed belief was displayed by his three Hebrew friends (Shadrach, Meshach, and Abednego), who entered a fiery furnace for what they believed and were found still standing.

The apostle Paul had that kind of belief. He was beaten for his faith in Christ; he was stoned and left for dead; he was imprisoned and eventually beheaded.

Read Paul's response to those persecutions in 2 Timothy 1:12. On what did Paul base his convictions?
- ❑ Whatever the prevailing culture said he should believe.
- ❑ Whatever his friends believed.
- ❑ His hope that God would deliver him from all harm.
- ❑ His belief in Who God is.

"I am not ashamed; for I know whom I have believed and I am convinced that He is able to guard what I have entrusted to Him until that day" (2 Tim. 1:12, NASB).

That's the kind of belief several students at Columbine High School had when guns were pointed at their heads and they were asked, "Do you believe in God?" And it cost them their lives.

Each of us is challenged to pursue that convinced, committed kind of belief in God and His Word. We need more than personal opinions or lightly held suspicions about God, truth, and reality; we need convictions. If each of us and our young people are going to risk rejection, persecution, or even worse, we need to be sure that we are committing our lives to something genuine, something true, something real.

Even in the face of persecution, the apostle Peter urged us to be prepared to explain the reason for our hope in Christ (1 Peter 3:9,13-15). And if each of us is going to develop the kind of convictions that enabled past generations to stand strong, our faith must be grounded in the objective truth and relational meaning of the things we believe. Only then will we—and our young people—move beyond mere belief to a set of convictions that will hold us steady in the battles of life.

> "Don't retaliate when people say unkind things about you. Instead, pay them back with a blessing. That is what God wants you to do, and he will bless you for it. Now, who will want to harm you if you are eager to do good? But even if you suffer for doing what is right, God will reward you for it. So don't be afraid and don't worry. Instead, you must worship Christ as Lord of your life. And if you are asked about your Christian hope, always be ready to explain it" (1 Pet. 3:9,13-15).

day Two

Convictions: Believing in What Is Objectively True

On the evening of September 10, 2001, nineteen young men read a prayer-laden letter regarding their last night on earth. "Be obedient on this night," the instructions in Arabic said, "because you will be facing situations that are the ultimate and that would not be done except with full obedience.... Then you will know all the heavens are decorated in the best way to meet you."

The next morning, on September 11, 2001, those nineteen young men gave their lives for what they believed in the worst terrorist attack in the history of the United States. They had a religious conviction that what they were doing was honoring to their god.

Those terrorists had deep convictions. From their point of view, they were advancing a just and holy war against evil in the world. They were convinced of "their" truth and were willing to die for it, though, understandably, most Americans were convinced that the terrorists were evil.

Osama bin Laden asserted one truth claim: God was on his side, and the terrorist acts were just. Most Americans, including the president of the

Week of JULY 25

United States, asserted another truth claim: God was on America's side, and the terrorists were "evildoers."

We know who was right, of course. We're convinced that what nineteen men did in killing more than three thousand people was evil. We're confident that Osama bin Laden wasn't acting righteously when he presumably ordered the deaths of innocent Americans.

But how do we know that? How can we be sure whose view of God and whose claims about truth are right? It is far more than a philosophical question—and the answer is far more than academic. Those terrorists are a vivid reminder that people can have deepened convictions and still be tragically wrong if the things they believe with conviction are *wrong beliefs*.

When faced with competing truth claims, the only way to arrive at a meaningful conclusion is by investigation. The careful observer must weigh the claims according to the evidence. If someone makes a claim that something is true, we ought to be able to "test" that claim to see if it is factually true and in accordance with the real world.

Read the following Scriptures. Fill in the blanks to create questions that test whether or not a conviction arises from a wrong belief.

Isaiah 8:20: Does this belief come from God's ____?

Matthew 7:18-20: What kind of _____ comes from the person holding this conviction?

John 5:23: Does the person who believes this way honor _____?

2 John 1:7: Does this person's belief system acknowledge _____?

If you desire to dig deeper . . .

Read the following Scriptures and create additional questions you can ask to test a belief.

- Deuteronomy 13:1-4
- Jeremiah 23:21
- Colossians 2:8
- 1 John 4:5

_____
_____
_____

THE FACTS OF THE MATTER

By examining the evidence about God and His Word, you and I and our youth can determine beyond a reasonable doubt that God's claims are objectively true. Christianity is a uniquely *factual* truth based on indisputable facts. It is a uniquely verifiable belief because it is based on historical facts that are clearly recognizable by and accessible to everyone. The central question, then, is this: Has the one true God, who is the source of the universe and all that is right and good, revealed Himself? And if so, can we know Him—and how can we do that?

A certain person in history revealed Himself to us and made an extraordinary truth claim. His name was Jesus; He said, "I am the way, the truth, and the life. No one can come to the Father except through me" (John 14:6). Jesus claimed to be God in the flesh. This claim can be tested by examining the evidences and checking the facts because the facts backing the claims of Christ are the cognitive, informational facts upon which all historical, legal, and ordinary decisions are based.

Read John 14:10-11. What facts did Jesus appeal to when He exhorted His disciples to believe He was the Son of the one true God? _____

The evidence was and is there to convince our minds that the claims of Christ are objectively true.

To move our kids beyond belief to conviction, therefore, we must guide them through an examination of the evidences for what they believe. Otherwise, neither they nor we will have a convinced belief that what we believe is objectively true. In that respect, it is healthy to require evidence of Christ's claims.

Have you ever examined why you believe what you believe? ❑ Yes ❑ No **Why or why not?** _____
_____

Ask God to give you the courage and spiritual insight to honestly examine what you believe so you can move beyond your beliefs to conviction.

The Necessity of Faith

I don't agree with those who suggest that the disciple Thomas did something terribly wrong when he insisted on seeing the evidence of Jesus' resurrection. Thomas wanted verification. He wanted to see the evidence before he committed to that belief.

Week of JULY 25

Read John 20:24-28 and answer the following:
Why do you think Thomas didn't merely want to see Jesus but wanted to put his hands in Jesus' wounds? _____

What invitation did Jesus issue Thomas? _____
Do you think Thomas took Jesus up on his offer?
❏ Yes ❏ No **Why or why not?** _____
What command did Jesus give Thomas? _____
How did Thomas respond to Jesus' command? _____
_____

I'm convinced we need more young Thomases—young people who know why they believe what they believe. Such understanding is a vital key in developing the right convictions.

The Bible itself repeatedly invites examination. The apostle John, who was there when Thomas saw the risen Christ, recorded that event and added: "Jesus' disciples saw him do many other miraculous signs besides the ones recorded in this book. But these are written so that you may believe that Jesus is the Messiah, the Son of God, and that by believing in him you will have life" (John 20:30-31).

John recorded some of the evidences that showed Jesus Christ to be the Son of the one true God so that we, like Thomas, could put faithlessness behind us and believe the objective truth with conviction.

Of course, no matter how thoroughly convincing the evidences are, we still must exercise faith. The faith Jesus calls for is not a blind faith but an informed, intelligent faith, one that is supported by evidence.

We will seldom, if ever, have exhaustive evidence, but we can find sufficient evidence to establish that what we believe is credible and objectively true. We also will seldom find that the evidence will remove all possibility of doubt. Life is filled with questions and circumstances that can test our faith and create momentary doubt.

A man who wanted Jesus to heal his son said to Christ, "'Have mercy on us and help us. Do something if you can.'

"'What do you mean, "If I can"?' Jesus asked. 'Anything is possible if a person believes.'

"The father instantly replied, 'I do believe, but help me not to doubt!'" (Mark 9:22-24).

Though this father believed in Jesus, he confessed that he needed help not to doubt. Even John the Baptist's faith seemed to waver when he was

Do you need to ask Jesus to help you overcome your disbelief?
❏ Yes ❏ No

Using the father's plea as an example, write a brief prayer below:

imprisoned and things were looking grim. He sent some of his followers to ask Jesus, "Are you really the Messiah we've been waiting for, or should we keep looking for someone else?" (Matthew 11:3).

Remember, this was the same man who, when he first saw Jesus, said, "Look! There is the Lamb of God who takes away the sin of the world! . . . He is the one you are looking for" (John 1:29-33). Yet, when John was arrested and thrown into prison, he must have wondered why this Jesus wasn't coming to his rescue. Like many of us in difficult times, John the Baptist experienced doubts.

> **Read Matthew 11:4-5. How did Jesus respond to John the Baptist's question?**
> ❑ He was insulted and refused to answer.
> ❑ He condemned John for his lack of faith.
> ❑ He enrolled John in a theology course.
> ❑ **He cited indisputable facts and events as evidence of His Messiahship.**

How did Jesus respond to John's questions? He pointed to indisputable facts and events. He told John's disciples,

Jesus reminded John of the *evidence*, the clear indications that Jesus was the Messiah. It was John's objective belief rooted in the reality of Christ as the Messiah that enabled him to stand strong even in the face of death. The trials of life often introduce temptation and doubt into our minds and hearts, but at such times the evidence can anchor us to the objective truth and confirm to us that what we believe is, in fact, true.

Examining the evidence doesn't eliminate the need for faith. No amount of evidence can create a 100 percent certainty. Believing something without evidence is like taking a leap into the dark; faith that is rooted in the truth is like stepping into the light. A faith that is rooted in the truth that we have reason to believe is objectively true will move us—and our kids—beyond belief to convictions in the one true God.

Leading our kids to a biblical Christianity that is shown to be objectively true is critical to a faith that will hold them firm and steady in the midst of a godless culture. Yet that is only one side of believing with convictions. The flip side is guiding them to understand the relational meaning of the things they believe.

"Go back to John and tell him about what you have heard and seen—the blind see, the lame walk, the lepers are cured, the deaf hear, the dead are raised to life, and the Good News is being preached to the poor"
(Matt. 11:4-5).

"Believing something without evidence is like taking a leap into the dark; faith that is rooted in the truth is like stepping into the light."
—Josh McDowell

Week of JULY 25

Convictions: Believing In What Is Relationally Meaningful

When Jesus invited His disciples to "believe because of what you have seen me do" (John 14:11), He referred not only to the evidences that make believing a rational, reasonable exercise but also to the context of the invitation. He invites us to believe in a *person*. Believing in Christ and His Word is to have a profound and *relational* meaning to each of our lives.

The vast majority of our kids see little correlation between the things they believe about God, truth, and reality and their relationships with friends and family, or their future in life. Remember, 74 percent of our kids are still trying to figure out the purpose and meaning of their lives, and 63 percent don't have a clear philosophy about life that consistently influences their lifestyle and decisions.

Because of the cultural mind-set that prompts today's youth to crave, even demand, what is "real, relevant, and right now," we have a golden opportunity. We can demonstrate not only what is *objectively true* about Christ and His Word but also the *relational meaning* of who Christ is and what He says to us through His Word, a meaning that meets their deepest relational needs and answers the most fundamental questions of life.

"Believe Me that I am in the Father and the Father is in Me. Otherwise, believe because of the works themselves" (John 14:11, HCSB).

> **Read John 10:10-15. Drawing from these verses and from your own convictions, how would you present Jesus to a person who demands what is:**
> **Real?** _____
> **Relevant?** _____
> **Right now?** _____

THE PERSON OF TRUTH
Moral and spiritual truth isn't so much a concept as it is a person. It isn't so much something we believe as it is someone to whom we relate. Moral and spiritual truth has flesh. Thus, truth is not just conceptual; it is intrinsically relational.

One definition of *truth* is "fidelity to an original or standard." When a carpenter says a floor or a wall is "true," he or she means that it's faithful to the original measurements. But what is the "original" or "standard" for transcendent truth, for the kind of truth Jesus talked about when He said, "I came to bring truth to the world" (John 18:37)? That standard is Jesus Himself.

If we wish to know if anything is right or wrong, good or evil, we must measure it against the person who is true. "He is the Rock," Moses said. "His work is perfect . . . a God of truth and without iniquity, just and right is he" (Deuteronomy 32:4, KJV). You see, the very person and nature of God defines truth. It is not something He measures up to or announces. It is not even something He decides. It is something He *is*.

This means that moral and spiritual truth isn't simply abstract or philosophical; it is best understood as a "who," not as a "what." And when we are careful to keep truth within that personal, relational context, it can change everything in the minds and hearts of our young people and the whole postmodern generation!

The apostle James was not talking in abstractions when he wrote: "Whatever is good and perfect comes to us from God above, who created all heaven's lights. Unlike them, he never changes or casts shifting shadows. In his goodness he chose to make us his own children by giving us his true word" (James 1:17-18).

God gave us the true Word—the one who said, "I came to bring truth to the world" (John 18:37)—for one purpose: to make us His own children. The Incarnate Truth came to this earth so we as the human race could be restored to full fellowship with our Father God. As the apostle John said, "The Word became flesh and made his dwelling among us. We have seen his glory, the glory of the One and Only, who came from the Father, full of grace *and truth*" (John 1:14, NIV, emphasis added).

Describe a time you acted on your beliefs regardless of the consequences.

Defining Convictions

As we've indicated, people can have convictions in misguided and wrong beliefs—as the terrorist attacks of September 11, 2001, prove. We must

Week of JULY 25

help our young people move beyond subjective believing to a conviction in what is objectively true. And those beliefs must be shown to be not only true but also relevant—that is, relationally meaningful to life.

Therefore, our task is to present the Christian faith to our young people in ways that demonstrate that believing is an intelligent exercise of knowing what is both objectively true and relationally meaningful. Having *convictions,* then, can be defined as *being so thoroughly convinced that Christ and His Word are both objectively true and relationally meaningful that you act on your beliefs regardless of the consequences.*

In the lessons that follow, we will offer what is needed to overcome our young people's distorted beliefs and lead them to the right kind of convictions. We will do this by providing a clear presentation of the most basic and foundational pillars of the Christian faith. And we will show why they are true and how they are meaningful to our lives.

A Light in the Midst of Darkness

I realize I've not presented a bright outlook on the task of moving our kids from belief to convictions. But while postmodernism may have created a cultural atmosphere in which convictions are taboo and evidences seem irrelevant, postmodernism also presents us with a unique opportunity.

The premium our kids place on community and relationships shines a bright light of hope on an otherwise dark set of circumstances. In a world in which convictions are not fashionable and evidences for truth irrelevant, we can capitalize on the culture's desire for relationships and focus on community. Because, as it so happens, the very nature of absolute truth is relational. It addresses our kids hunger for relationships that really do work. It can answer their heartfelt cry for community, connectedness, and a sense of belonging. Because truth—absolute truth—is intensely and unavoidably relational.

> "Truth—absolute truth—is intensely and unavoidably relational."
> —Josh McDowell

Read John 6:66-69.
What objective truth about Jesus did Peter state? _____

How did he express that truth in terms of a meaningful relationship with Christ? _____

What relevant needs of the disciples were met by their intimate relationship with the Son of God? _____

NOTES

To the Leader:

"But you have an anointing from the Holy One, and all of you know the truth. I do not write to you because you do not know the truth, but because you do know it" (1 John 2:20-21, NIV).

Ask the Holy Spirit to anoint you as you prepare to teach this week. Determine to present objective truth through careful study of God's Word. Also seek to present the Person of Truth by demonstrating to your class through words, actions, and attitudes, your intimate personal relationship with Christ.

Before the Session

1. Find a true story about a present day persecuted Christian. Stories can be found at www.opendoorsusa.org or you can do an internet search using the key words "persecuted church."
2. Read "During the Session." Choose and study the steps you will use in your lesson plan.
3. Write the "convictions" definition (in italics, Day 5) on a poster.

During the Session

1. Relate the story about a present-day persecuted believer. Inquire where a person obtains that kind of courage. Note the believer had moved beyond belief to convictions. Ask learners to describe the difference between beliefs and convictions.
2. Invite a volunteer to read Daniel 3:16-18. Ask participants to state what the three young men believed. [That God could deliver them.] Request they state the young men's conviction. [God was the only true God worthy of worship.] Ask: *Do you agree or disagree that our convictions must be based on who God is rather than on what God does for us? Why or why not?*
3. Ask if adults think persecution accompanies true convictions and why. Comment that the 1 Peter passage in Day 1 gives instructions to respond positively to persecution. Request a volunteer read that passage aloud. Ask learners to turn to Daniel 6 in their Bibles and follow along as you read Daniel 6:3-23. Instruct them to interrupt you each time you read an instance from Daniel's experience that illustrates the principles taught in 1 Peter 3. [Examples: suffer for doing what is right; don't retaliate; worship Christ as Lord; always be ready to explain your hope.]
4. Ask: *What did Dr. McDowell declare are the two essential elements to believing with convictions?* Draw a line down the middle of a writing surface. Write "Objective Truth" at the top of one column and "Relational Meaning" at the other.
5. Write "Wrong beliefs" in the Objective Truth column and ask, *How is it possible to believe absolutely and still be absolutely wrong?* Invite

Week of JULY 25

volunteers to share the questions they created in Day 2 to help them test whether a conviction arises from a wrong belief. Use the Scriptures in the margin to create additional questions to test claims of truth. Ask: *Does it really matter what you believe, as long as you believe in something? Why?* To discover the end results of holding wrong beliefs, ask two volunteers to read Job 15:31 and Isaiah 5:20.

6. Ask, *On what must objective truth be based?* Write "Evidence" in the "Objective Truth" column. Guide the class to discuss the first activity in Day 3. Ask: *Do you think it is wrong to require evidence? Why?* Comment that it is wrong to still not believe after valid evidence is given. Ask learners to read John 20:29 silently to discover how Jesus feels about those who believe without seeing physical evidence.

7. Ask someone to read the quotation in the margin on page 102. Ask, *How would you respond to the comment "Christianity is a blind faith"?* Invite volunteers to share evidences about Jesus that have anchored them, especially in turbulent times.

8. Ask, *If objective truth is based on evidence, what is relational meaning based on?* Write responses in the Relational Meaning column. [Possible answers might be: An intimate relationship with God. What is real, relevant, and right now.] Request volunteers share their responses to the first activity in Day 4.

9. Request someone read aloud the quotation in the margin on page 105. Ask: *Can you know absolute truth if you do not have an intentional and intense relationship with Christ? Why or why not?*

10. Display the "convictions" poster and read it aloud. Recall the story of the persecuted Christian related earlier in the lesson. Ask, *How did that person live out the definition of having convictions?* Invite volunteers to relate other situations where a believer's convictions were so strong that he or she acted regardless of the consequences. Ask: *Why must that kind of faith be based on objective truth <u>and</u> on a personal relationship with Christ? How can we present the relational side of truth to our world?*

After the Session

1. Read next week's lesson and complete the learning activities.
2. Strive to build a relationship with a new member or visitor. Meet for lunch or sit together at a fellowship meal.

NOTES

The Truth about Truth

What Is Truth?

Nearly twenty centuries ago, a high government official, trained in politics and the law, asked a question that has echoed all the way into the twenty-first century.

I can see Pontius Pilate, then the Roman governor of Judea, standing in his elaborate palace, bedecked in regal clothes, questioning the shackled prisoner who had been brought before him.

"Are you the King of the Jews?" Pilate asks the prisoner accused of sedition.

This prisoner, unlike most, stands straight in the presence of the governor and looks him in the eyes when He speaks. "I am not an earthly king. My kingdom is not of this world."

"You *are* a king then?" the governor says.

"*You* say that I am a king," the prisoner answers, aware that His interrogator is in a prickly political position, "and you are right." The prisoner looks at the politician with eyes that seem to read the expression not only on his face but of his soul as well. "I was born for that purpose," He goes on, "and I came to bring truth to the world. All who love the truth recognize that what I say is true."

Read John 18:38. Pilate responded, "____ ___ _____?"

I want you to imagine for a moment that you are in that hall with Pilate and his prisoner. Imagine the words of the governor's question echoing off the marbled walls of that great hall. Imagine the expression on Pilate's face as he poses the question, scornful at first, then turning serious when the answer does not quickly come.

Seconds tick by. Still the prisoner and the governor study each other. Imagine the governor's thoughts: *Who is this man? Why does He gaze at me so?*

Week of AUGUST 1

And the prisoner's thoughts: *Have I not just told you? I came to bring truth to the world. Pilate, you are looking at the answer to your own question:* I *am the truth.*

Earlier in His ministry Jesus told His disciples: "You will know the truth, and the truth will set you free" (John 8:32). And just a few moments later, Jesus made clear that the truth He had in mind was not only a concept but also a person, when He said: "So if the Son sets you free, you will indeed be free" (John 8:36).

> **Read John 8:32 and 8:36 again. Was Jesus confused when He first stated the truth set people free and then claimed the Son set people free?**
> ❏ Yes ❏ No ❏ Not Sure   Explain. _____

Jesus was not speaking in riddles. He is the one who said, "I am the way, *the truth,* and the life" (John 14:6, emphasis added). Jesus is the very embodiment of truth.

This is an important realization in our postmodern age—and particularly among our young people, who place such emphasis on relationships and community. They need to understand that truth is not simply an abstract concept; it is not something we create within ourselves. They need to see that truth is intrinsically, inescapably relational because it resides in and springs from a person who loves them and desires a relationship with them, person to person, friend to friend.

A Shift from "What" to "Who"

To counter our young people's faulty thinking about truth—that all moral and spiritual truth is subjective and equal—we must shift the emphasis. "What we believe" must be seen in the context of "who we believe." Believing in Christ is about forming a relationship with a real person. Therefore, how we relate to the Person of Truth must become the central issue.

This shift from "what" to "who" will mean a major shift in how we think of Christianity and how we teach our kids the Christian faith. How we relate

If you desire to dig deeper . . .

Read the following Scriptures. Note ways these biblical instructions can help you develop a deeper relationship with Christ.
- **Galatians 6:1-10**
- **Ephesians 4:25–5:1**
- **Philippians 2:1-5**
- **Colossians 3:1-17**

to moral and spiritual truth should no longer be thought of merely as a philosophical concept or abstract idea but rather how we relate to a person. Scriptural commands and rules should no longer be seen as merely instructions to obey but rather as ways to relate to a person. As we embrace the realization that Jesus is the embodiment of truth and explain the Christian faith as a life lived in relationship with God through Christ, we can counter our young people's faulty perceptions of God, truth, and reality.

Read Exodus 20:1-17, not as rules to obey but as instructions for forming a personal relationship with God. What do His Ten Commandments say to you?

Understanding Jesus Christ as the absolute embodiment of truth means:
- Truth could not be subjectively created; truth is and comes from the objective, absolute person of Christ Himself. As John wrote: "For the law was given through Moses; grace and truth came through Jesus Christ" (John 1:17, NIV).
- Truth could not be relative and change from person to person, from community to community, because Jesus is the incarnation of the God who "never changes or casts shifting shadows" (James 1:17). As the Scripture says: "Jesus Christ is the same yesterday, today, and forever" (Hebrews 13:8).
- All truth could not be equal because Jesus didn't claim to be "a" truth, one that is equal to all others. His claim was exclusive; He claimed to be the one and only truth, the only way to God. "I am *the* way, *the* truth, and *the* life," He said. "No one can come to the Father except through me" (John 14:6, emphasis added). Those are not the words of someone who is "one among many," someone who is "equal" to all others; those are the words of one who has no equal.

This, then, is what we must do to lead our young people beyond belief to conviction. We must transform their mistaken, misguided perceptions of truth by leading them to encounter the one and only true Person of Truth—Jesus Christ. Then we can point our young people to the historical evidence that establishes Jesus Christ as the one and only true and perfect God of the universe.

So the next step in this process is to look at what will convince our young people that Christ is the Son of the one true God.

Week of AUGUST 1

Which statement best describes your role in leading young people beyond belief to conviction?
- ❑ That's the youth minister's job.
- ❑ I'm completely inadequate but willing for God to use me.
- ❑ I'm excited about the prospect and can't wait to get started.
- ❑ I'm already involved in leading young people from belief to conviction and am reaping the rewards.

Christ's Teachings or Christ's Identity?

Educators commonly tell their students that Jesus made His *teachings* the central issue and that He never made a claim to deity. The problem with this idea is that it is not true.

Jesus *did* claim to be the Son of God, and that claim was central to everything else He said and did.

> Read Matthew 16:13-17 and complete the following:
> What did Jesus ask the disciples? _____
> How would most 21st century persons answer that question? _____
> What is the difference between Jesus' questions in verses 13 and 15? _____
> How did Jesus' response to Peter affirm His deity? _____

According to the New Testament record, Jesus repeatedly made it clear that He was the unique Son of God, an assertion that did not go unnoticed by the religious leaders of His day. In fact, that was the very reason they tried to discredit and, eventually, put Him to death: "So the Jewish leaders tried all the more to kill him. In addition to disobeying the Sabbath rules, he had spoken of God as his Father, thereby making himself equal with God" (John 5:18).

On more than one occasion, Jesus' clear assertion of His own deity caused His fellow Jews to want to stone Him. Once, when He told the

Jewish leaders, "Your father Abraham rejoiced at the thought of seeing my day; he saw it and was glad," His listeners became indignant: "You are not yet fifty years old,' the Jews said to him, 'and you have seen Abraham!'

"'I tell you the truth,' Jesus answered, 'before Abraham was born, I am!' At this, they picked up stones to stone him, but Jesus hid himself, slipping away from the temple grounds" (John 8:56-59, NIV).

Read Exodus 3:13-14. Why did Jesus' choice of words make the Jews so furious? _____

> "'I and the Father are one.' Again the Jews picked up stones to stone him, but Jesus said to them, 'I have shown you many great miracles from the Father. For which of these do you stone me?' 'We are not stoning you for any of these,' replied the Jews, 'but for blasphemy, because you, a mere man, claim to be God'"
> (John 10:30-33, NIV).

On another occasion, when Jesus said that He was one with the Father, the Jewish leaders again picked up stones to kill Him.

Read John 10:30-33 in the margin. Underline the reason the Jews wanted to stone Jesus.

Yet another time, Jesus told a paralyzed man, "My son, your sins are forgiven" and again the religious leaders reacted with outrage. "What?" they said. "This is blasphemy! *Who but God* can forgive sins!" (Mark 2:5-7, emphasis added).

In the final days prior to Jesus' death, He made it clear—even to the Sanhedrin (the Jewish high council)—just who He was: "Then the high priest asked Him, 'Are you the Messiah, the Son of the blessed God?' Jesus said, 'I am.'" In response to the proclamation, they "condemned him to death" (Mark 14:61-64).

Take a few moments to list in the margin the highlights of what you recall Jesus saying and doing while He was on earth.
Why must His claim to be God be true if those words and actions are to have any lasting meaning?
_____

The central issue of Christianity is not the teachings of a man called Jesus but the person of Jesus Christ Himself. And throughout the Gospel record, Jesus urged His listeners and followers to believe *in Him,* not just in His teachings (see John 3:15-16; 8:24; 11:25; 12:46; 20:29).

In fact, the identity of Jesus is utterly crucial to understanding everything He had to say. All that Jesus said and did pointed to His identity as the Messiah, the Son of God, and to the purpose for which He came to

Week of AUGUST 1

earth. If He is not who He claimed to be, then His teachings are either the ramblings of a lunatic who sincerely *thought* He was God (but wasn't) or the words of a liar who *knew* He wasn't God (but said He was). If His claims are true, however, then He is not a liar or a lunatic—He is Lord!

But can we know whether or not Jesus' claim to be God is true? How can any of our kids, or any of us, be sure that Jesus Christ is the Son of the one true God?

There is a way. Jesus did not make His claims to deity without also providing sufficient evidence to support His claims. And, more than that, the evidence Jesus provided—in the fulfillment of messianic prophecies, the Virgin Birth, and the miracles—is so overwhelming and compelling that it ought to fill our hearts and souls with awe and wonder at the God-man, Jesus Christ. We will examine these lines of evidence in the next lesson.

In your opinion, what is the difference between merely believing Jesus' teachings and believing in Jesus?

___

Do you believe Jesus . . .
___ **is a legendary figure?**
___ **was a good man?**
___ **was an extraordinary teacher?**
___ **was God in human form?**

day Four

God Makes His Move

Imagine God as He watches in grief and sadness while you are born into the very world where He and Adam once walked in perfect relationship. He longs to relate to you as intimately as He once did to Adam and Eve. He wants to take pleasure in you. He wants to see in your eyes the delight that only His life and love can bring you. But that's not possible because you have been dead to Him, separated from the life that is found in Him. God has been watching from the very first moments of your life as you follow in Adam and Eve's footsteps, becoming His *enemy* by repeatedly and selfishly choosing your own sinful ways instead of God's holy ways.

> "We all, like sheep, have gone astray, each of us has turned to his own way" (Isa. 53:6a).
>
> **According to Isaiah 53:6a, how has your life resembled a straying sheep?**
>
> _____
>
> **Read Luke 19:10. What does Jesus do about straying sheep?**
>
> _____
>
> **Read the last half of Isaiah 53:6 in your Bible. How does Jesus save His sheep?**
>
> _____
>
> **Read Isaiah 53:4-10 in your Bible. Record some of the extraordinary lengths to which Jesus went to have a personal relationship with you.**
>
> _____
>
> _____

So God made His move. *He* took the initiative. You are the one who desperately needs Him, but *you* didn't seek *Him* out. So He enters your world to cancel the curse of death that has power over you. "Because God's children are human beings—made of flesh and blood—Jesus also became flesh and blood by being born in human form. For only as a human being could he die, and only by dying could he break the power of the Devil, who had the power of death" (Hebrews 2:14). Only the Son of the living God could wrench the power of death out of the hand of Satan so God could be reconnected to all creation in a personal, one-on-one relationship.

Through the Incarnation of Jesus Christ God says, "You may have turned away from Me, but I'm not turning away from you. You are so important to Me that I will go to extraordinary lengths to have a personal relationship with you. I'll enter your world and become human like you to save you from death and eternal aloneness without Me."

That is so important for us—and our kids—to realize. The core of Christianity is far, far more than a set of true propositions; it is the news of "a God *who is passionate about his relationship with you*" (Exodus 34:14, emphasis added), offering us eternal life and relationship with Him through the Incarnate One—Jesus Christ.

Every word God has spoken, every command He has given, every action He has taken has been a means to an end. Behind God's plan to conquer death is His desire to enjoy an everlasting and personal relationship with you, your children, friends, and loved ones. The Incarnation shows God's love in action, providing a way to achieve that personal relationship, a relationship that gives you life and restores your true identity as a priceless human being created in God's image. The Incarnation demonstrates God's desire to have a relationship with you—but the relationship God has in mind is not simply some casual acquaintance but one that relates to you on a deep and intimate level.

> **Read Zephaniah 3:16-17. Seek to grasp how precious you are to God by filling in the blanks.**
>
> **Do not fear, _____ (your name), do not let your hands hang limp. For the Lord your God is _____ you, He is mighty to _____.**
> **He takes _____ _____ in you,**
> **He will _____ you with His _____**
> **He will _____ over you with _____.**

Week of AUGUST 1

The Relational Meaning of the Incarnation

There are at least four expressions that characterize God's relationship to you—He accepts you unconditionally, loves you sacrificially, understands you intimately, and relates to you continuously.

1. God Accepts You Unconditionally

Name one person who loves you without a single condition. _____

Were you able to write a single name? _____

God's divine passion to relate to you and enter your world isn't based on anything you have done or could do in the future. It is purely the result of God's grace (see Ephesians 2:8). It was extended to you, a sinner and an enemy of God, while you were gripped by death (see Romans 5:8-12). Regardless of all you've done—or haven't done—He offers grace. *God accepts you* completely, and in spite of your sin He provides a way back to Him.

The gospel story is about Christ, who took the initiative and entered our world when we were helpless, unable to even ask for help, and showed us grace—favor that was not merited at all.

Are you ready to enter the life God desires to share with you through the grace He freely offers you?
❏ Yes   ❏ No   ❏ Not Sure
Turn to the front inside cover of this publication and discover how you can begin a life-changing relationship with God.

2. God Loves You Sacrificially

God has demonstrated that He is willing to go to extraordinary lengths to connect with you. But God is not only a God who is "rich in mercy"

How can the death sentence against sinners be abolished?
_____

Can we save ourselves? Read Romans 5:6. ❏ Yes ❏ No
Why? _____

Can the Law save us? Read Romans 8:3. ❏ Yes ❏ No
Why? _____

What is the only thing that can save us?
_____

"This is real love . . . that [God] loved us and sent his Son as a sacrifice to take away our sins" (1 John 4:10).

Draw a symbol of real love.

Why did you choose that symbol?
_____

Have you had someone in your life who understands and identifies with you? Write his or her name here.
_____

Spend a moment thanking God for the gift of that person.

(Ephesians 2:4). He is also holy. God is so holy that He "cannot allow sin in any form" (Habakkuk 1:13).

Since each of us are tainted by sin, we are totally unsuitable for a relationship with a holy God. Therefore, even though God's mercy prompts Him to accept us, His holiness requires that our sinfulness be dealt with.

But how? We cannot save ourselves. Because God is not only holy but also just, He solved the problem in a way that satisfied both His holiness and His justice. The penalty of sin had to be paid: "The wages of sin is death" (Romans 6:23). A sacrifice was needed, but not just any sacrifice would do. In His holiness God would accept only a pure, spotless, sinless sacrifice. But no one on earth—no one in the history of humanity—could fill that bill.

So, what could be done? "God put into effect a different plan to save us. He sent his own Son in a human body like ours, except that ours are sinful. God destroyed sin's control over us by giving his Son as a sacrifice for our sins" (Romans 8:3). "God sent Jesus to take the punishment for our sins" (Romans 3:25). Jesus Christ, God incarnate, who knew no sin and was undeserving of any punishment—became sin on our behalf. Jesus Christ became the atoning sacrifice for your sins and mine.

The truth of the Incarnation reveals that God so desires a relationship with you that He made the ultimate sacrifice—for you. *God loves you and longs to relate to you.* He proved it by becoming human Himself and laying down His life for you.

3. God Understands You Intimately

We all long for someone to understand and identify with us, especially when life seems hard or confusing or unfair.

The Incarnation—the truth that God had become human—means that Christ understands us. He understands everything we have ever endured—and more. The Incarnate One, Jesus Christ, experienced the ups and downs of life as a human baby, child, teenager, and man. He suffered embarrassment, humiliation, and rejection—and more.

Because Christ took on human form, we can know that He truly understands our weaknesses and temptations. The writer of Hebrews tells us that Christ "has gone through suffering and temptation . . . [and] is able to help us when we are being tempted. . . . [He] understands our weaknesses, for he faced all of the same temptations we do, yet he did not sin."

Week of AUGUST 1

So let us come boldly . . . and we will find grace to help us when we need it" (Hebrews 2:18; 4:15-16). There is nothing you have experienced that God in Christ does not understand firsthand! The Incarnation is Jesus' way of saying, "I understand," no matter what emotion you may be feeling, no matter what experience you may be enduring.

Do you honestly believe Jesus completely understands you? ❏ Yes ❏ No ❏ Not Sure
If you answered No, pray for your eyes to be opened and your relationship with Christ to be strengthened. If you answered Yes, how has your relationship with Christ been deepened by that understanding? _____

Read the following Scriptures and note how Jesus' life experiences were similar to your experiences.
- Luke 2:6-7
- Luke 2:42-52
- Luke 4:1-2
- Matthew 13:53-57
- Matthew 14:9-13
- Mark 3:20-21
- Mark 14:43-45
- Luke 22:60-61

4. God Relates to You Continually

When Jesus approached the conclusion of His three-year ministry on earth, His disciples—His closest friends on earth—struggled to understand His talk about leaving them.

Read John 14:16-19 in the margin. How did Jesus explain to His followers that He would continue to relate to them? _____

By dying, rising from the dead, and ascending into heaven again God made all the affection, acceptance, and affirmation of Jesus available to us every moment of our lives through the constant, indwelling presence of the Comforter, His Holy Spirit. "For we know how dearly God loves us, because he has given us the Holy Spirit to fill our hearts with his love" (Romans 5:5). That is how Jesus delivers on His promise "I am with you always, even to the end of the age" (Matthew 28:20). Jesus is available to us, anywhere, anytime, and all the time.

You see, contrary to the way many of our kids—and some of us—have learned to think of Him, Jesus Christ is not some distant historical figure who lived two thousand years ago. He actually enters our very being to become one with us. Now that's a close relationship!

"I will ask the Father, and he will give you another Counselor, who will never leave you. He is the Holy Spirit, who leads into all truth. . . . He lives with you now and later will be in you. No, I will not abandon you as orphans—I will come to you. In just a little while the world will not see me again, but you will. For I will live again, and you will, too" (John 14:16-19).

Do you think of Jesus more as
___ a distant historical figure?
___ a constant companion?
___ an indwelling presence of God?

NOTES

To the Leader:

Evaluate your class's outreach ministry. Who is contacting prospects and absentee members?

You may consider asking several members to take on this ministry on a rotating basis. Provide them with names, phone numbers, and addresses.

This week, strive to contact each person on your outreach list yourself—a 5-minute phone call could make a tremendous difference in an adult's life.

Before the Session

1. Request four volunteers to be prepared to read John 1:10-13; 17:1-5; Hebrews 1:1-3; and 2:9-11.
2. Read "During the Session." Choose the teaching steps you will use.

During the Session

1. Welcome participants. Open with prayer requests and prayer.
2. As a review for all learners and to enlighten those who are attending this study for the first time, ask participants to explain what it means to move beyond beliefs to convictions. You may refer to the "convictions" poster you displayed last week. Review the two essential elements to believing with conviction. [Objective truth and Relational meaning]
3. Ask: *How would you answer if someone asked you, "What is truth?" Why must we present truth to young people as a relationship with the Person of Christ rather than just objective facts?* Invite volunteers to share their responses to the first activity in Day 2. Ask: *How would your approach to Bible study be different if you viewed all scriptural commands as a way to relate to the Person of Christ rather than just as instructions to obey?* Working all together or in smaller groups, read the Scriptures listed in the margin on page 109; make a list of instructions to obey found in each passage; then discuss how those rules can lead a person to a deeper relationship with Christ.
4. Read Matthew 16:13-17. Request volunteers share their response to the first activity in Day 3. Inquire, *Others through history have claimed to be God; what makes Jesus' claim genuine?* Ask someone to read Matthew 26:59-66. Comment that Jesus didn't back off His claim to divinity even though it led to His being condemned to death.
5. Invite volunteers to share their responses to the last activity on page 112. Request the four enlisted volunteers read their Scripture passages. Discuss how these passages help explain why Jesus' claim of deity must be central to His ministry and message.
6. Read John 8:23-25. Lead a discussion on the difference between believing Jesus' teachings and believing in Jesus.

Week of AUGUST 1

7. Ask: *How does the passage from Isaiah 53 studied in the margin of Day 4 [p. 114] not only describe the great lengths Jesus went to save you, but also serve as evidence that He truly is God?* [He was the fulfillment of that prophecy.]
8. Remind the class that not only is Jesus God, He also is fully human. Ask: *Why is Jesus' humanity just as crucial to His mission as His deity? Why did He have to die to break sin's hold over humanity?* To help answer those questions, ask someone to read Hebrews 2:14-15.
9. Ask, *What must we do to get God to love us so much He will seek a relationship with us?* Request volunteers read aloud Romans 5:8-10 and 1 Corinthians 1:26-28 and lead the class to describe what they were like when Christ died for them. Ask, *How does this help you understand that God loves you unconditionally?*
10. Read aloud Romans 8:32. Comment, *If God sent His Son to die for us when we were totally unlovable, imagine what He will do to maintain that relationship with us once we belong to His family!* Then ask: *Do you think the problem of sin is the only problem we have that we need God to solve? Why?* Guide adults to understand that because of Christ's sacrifice believers can have a relationship with God that allows them to call on Him for all of their problems.
11. Ask, *How can we know Christ understands and cares about our problems?* Invite volunteers to share how Christ's life experiences were similar to their own. [See the activity in the margin on p. 117.] Ask participants to name experiences Jesus endured that go beyond anything they have endured. Ask, *Why did He endure such?* Allow volunteers to share what they sketched in the margin on page 116 to symbolize real love and have them tell why.
12. Ask learners how Jesus fulfilled His promise of Matthew 28:20. [the Holy Spirit] Have members state what role the Holy Spirit plays in their lives as believers.
13. Close in prayer, thanking Jesus for going to such great lengths to restore a relationship with humanity. Ask for courage to stand on your convictions so you can help bring others into a relationship with God.

After the Session

1. Read next week's lesson and complete the learning activities.
2. Work with class leaders to plan a potluck after church one Sunday.

NOTES

Proofs of Christ's Deity

Messianic Prophecies Fulfilled in One Person

Imagine God, several millennia ago, devising the plan to send His only Son to earth to be born as a human infant.

If we could have spoken down the corridors of time, we might have asked, "How will we know Him? How will we recognize Him as the Messiah, the eternal, incarnate Son of God?"

God might have responded, "I will cause Him to be born as an Israelite, a descendant of Abraham (Genesis 22:18; Galatians 3:16)."

"But," we might have protested, "Abraham's descendants will be as numerous as the stars!"

"Then I will narrow it down to only half of Abraham's lineage, and make Him a descendant of Isaac, not Ishmael (Genesis 21:12; Luke 3:23-34)."

"That will help, but isn't that still an awful lot of people?"

"Let him be born from Jacob's line, then, eliminating half of Isaac's lineage (Numbers 24:17; Luke 3:23-34)."

"But—"

"I will be more specific. Jacob will have twelve sons; I will bring forth the Messiah from the tribe of Judah (Genesis 49:10; Luke 3:23-33)."

"Won't that still be a lot of people? We still may not recognize Him when He comes."

"Don't worry! Look for Him in the family line of Jesse (Isaiah 11:1; Luke 3:23-32). *And* from the house and lineage of Jesse's youngest son, David (Jeremiah 23:5; Luke 3:23-31). And then I will tell you *where* He

> "Now Jesus . . . was the son . . . of David, the son of Jesse . . . the son of Judah, the son of Jacob, the son of Isaac, the son of Abraham . . . the son of Adam, the son of God" (Luke 3:23,31,34,37).

Week of AUGUST 8

will be born: Bethlehem, a tiny town in the area called Judah (Micah 5:2; Matthew 2:1)."

"But how will we know which person born there is your Son?"

"Read the following Old Testament prophecies and their corresponding New Testament fulfillments. Then, judging from what you learn about the Messiah in these verses, how do you think I would answer your question?"

1. Isaiah 40:3 and Matthew 3:1-3 _____

_____

2. Isaiah 9:1 and Matthew 4:12-16 _____

_____

3. Psalm 78:2 and Matthew 13:34-35 _____

_____

4. Isaiah 35:5-6 and Matthew 9:35 _____

_____

"Okay, that should help a lot."

"Oh," God might have responded, "I'm just getting warmed up. He will ride into the city of Jerusalem on a donkey (Zechariah 9:9; Matthew 21:2; Luke 19:35-37) and will appear suddenly and forcefully at the temple courts and zealously 'clean house' (Psalm 69:9; Malachi 3:1; John 2:15-16). Why, in *one day* I will fulfill no fewer than *twenty-nine* specific prophecies spoken at least five hundred years earlier about Him!

"Listen to this—

1. He will be betrayed by a friend (Psalm 41:9; Matthew 26:49).
2. The price of His betrayal will be thirty pieces of silver (Zechariah 11:12; Matthew 26:15).
3. His betrayal money will be cast to the floor of my temple (Zechariah 11:13; Matthew 27:5).
4. His betrayal money will be used to buy the potter's field (Zechariah 11:13; Matthew 27:7).
5. He will be forsaken and deserted by His disciples (Zechariah 13:7; Mark 14:50).

6. He will be accused by false witnesses (Psalm 35:11; Matthew 26:59-60).
7. He will be silent before His accusers (Isaiah 53:7; Matthew 27:12).
8. He will be wounded and bruised (Isaiah 53:5; Matthew 27:26).
9. He will be hated without a cause (Psalm 69:4; John 15:25).
10. He will be struck and spit on (Isaiah 50:6; Matthew 26:67).
11. He will be mocked, ridiculed, and rejected (Isaiah 53:3; Matthew 27:27-31; and John 7:5,48).
12. He will collapse from weakness (Psalm 109:24-25; Luke 23:26).
13. He will be taunted with specific words (Psalm 22:6-8; Matthew 27:39-43).
14. People will shake their heads at Him (Psalm 109:25; Matthew 27:39).
15. People will stare at Him (Psalm 22:17; Luke 23:35).
16. He will be executed among 'sinners' (Isaiah 53:12; Matthew 27:38).
17. His hands and feet will be pierced (Psalm 22:16; Luke 23:33).
18. He will pray for His persecutors (Isaiah 53:12; Luke 23:34).
19. His friends and family will stand afar off and watch (Psalm 38:11; Luke 23:49).
20. His garments will be divided and won by the casting of lots (Psalm 22:18; John 19:23-24).
21. He will thirst (Psalm 69:21; John 19:28).
22. He will be given gall and vinegar (Psalm 69:21; Matthew 27:34).
23. He will commit Himself to God (Psalm 31:5; Luke 23:46).
24. His bones will be left unbroken (Psalm 34:20; John 19:33).
25. His heart will rupture (Psalm 22:14; John 19:34).
26. His side will be pierced (Zechariah 12:10; John 19:34).
27. Darkness will come over the land at midday (Amos 8:9; Matthew 27:45).
28. He will be buried in a rich man's tomb (Isaiah 53:9; Matthew 27:57-60).
29. He will die 483 years after the declaration of Artaxerxes to rebuild the temple in 444 B.C. (Daniel 9:24).
30. As a final testimony, on the third day after His death, He will be raised from the dead (Psalm 16:10; Acts 2:31), ascend to heaven (Psalm 68:18; Acts 1:9), and be seated at the right hand of God in full majesty and authority (Psalm 110:1; Hebrews 1:3)."

Week of AUGUST 8

What extraordinary lengths God went to in order to help people identify and recognize His only begotten Son! Jesus fulfilled sixty major Old Testament prophecies (with about 270 additional ramifications)—all of which were made more than 400 years before His birth. This makes a compelling case for the deity of Christ.

Identify an event in your life for which you spent a great deal of time and effort in preparation.

_____

What did your efforts into planning say about the importance of this event to you?

_____

What does the amount of time and preparation God put into making His incarnate Son recognizable to humanity say to you personally?

_____

The Probability Factor

Read the question posed to Jesus in Mark 14:61. Write the initials "HP" on the scale below to indicate whether you think the high priest asked this question honestly or skeptically. On the same scale, write the initials of a person (perhaps yourself) who is asking that same question about Jesus.

|—————|—————|—————|—————|

Honest   **Skeptical**

"Then the high priest asked him, 'Are you the Messiah, the Son of the blessed God?'" (Mark 14:61, NLT).

Yet we must admit that Jesus was not the only Jew to be born into the tribe of Judah, in the city of Bethlehem, and buried in a rich man's tomb. Is it possible to believe that some of the details of Jesus' life just happened to coincide with all those Old Testament prophecies?

For the answer to that question, we need only turn to the science of statistics and probabilities. Professor Peter W. Stoner, in an analysis that was carefully reviewed and pronounced to be sound by the American Scientific Affiliation, states that the probability of just *eight* prophecies being fulfilled in one person is 1 in 10^{17} (that's 1 in 100,000,000,000,000,000).

Look at it this way: If you were to take 100,000,000,000,000,000 silver dollars and spread them across the state of Texas, they would not only cover the entire state but also form a pile of coins two feet deep! Now, take one more silver dollar, mark it with a big red *X*, toss it into that pile, and stir the whole pile thoroughly.

Then, blindfold yourself, and starting at El Paso on the western border of the state, walk the length and breadth of that enormous state, from Amarillo in the panhandle to Laredo on the Rio Grande all the way to Galveston on the Gulf of Mexico, stooping just once along the way to pick up a single silver dollar out of that two-foot-deep pile. Then take off your blindfold, and look at the silver dollar in your hand. What are the chances that you would pick up the marked coin out of a pile of silver dollars the size of the Lone Star State? *The same chance that one person could have fulfilled just eight messianic prophecies in one lifetime.*

In other words, it is nearly unthinkable to imagine that eight Old Testament prophecies about the Messiah could have come true in one man—let alone the *sixty* major prophecies that were fulfilled in Jesus of Nazareth—unless, of course, He *is* (as He Himself claimed) "the Messiah, the Son of the blessed God," the one who was and is and is to come (Mark 14:61; Revelation 4:8).

How did today's study help you appreciate the fact that Jesus was God's promised Messiah?

It didn't help at all because _____

It helped greatly because _____

Week of AUGUST 8

The Virgin Birth

Long before the prophets spoke, before anyone had heard of the Messiah, God erected in the Garden of Eden a signpost that pointed directly to the means by which His Son would be born. God's merciful and masterful plan to restore His relationship with the human family that had turned from Him was to enter the human family Himself and take the form of a man. God's declaration was made in the wake of Adam and Eve's original sin, in the very first words of judgment God spoke into earth's atmosphere. When God cursed the serpent who tempted Eve, He said: "And from now on, you and the woman will be enemies, and your offspring and her offspring will be enemies. He [Christ] will crush your head, and you will strike his heel" (Genesis 3:15).

The natural process of conceiving and giving birth involves the egg of a woman and the sperm, the "seed" of a man. But God, as recorded in Genesis 3:15, referred to a *supernatural* process when He promised that the serpent, Satan, would be defeated by the seed of a woman—not the seed of any man.

Scripture foretold that same supernatural process again, seven hundred years before God was born as a child, when the prophet Isaiah said, "The Lord himself will choose the sign. Look! The virgin will conceive a child! She will give birth to a son and will call him Immanuel—'God is with us'" (Isaiah 7:14).

What striking words: "the *virgin* will *conceive*." In the course of nature, virgins don't conceive. Conception requires fertilization of the female's ovum (egg) by the male's gamete (sperm) to form a new cell, called a zygote. The zygote must then implant itself in the lining of the uterus. That single cell then possesses a complete set of chromosomes, having received half its genetic information from each parent—all the information that will guide its development as a new, distinct, individual is being formed.

But God, speaking to the serpent, and again through the prophet Isaiah, promised something that human history had never seen before (or since):

> "God's merciful and masterful plan to restore His relationship with the human family that had turned from Him was to enter the human family Himself."
> —Josh McDowell

A child would be born outside the natural process of conception. Instead, the Holy Spirit of God Himself would form, in the dark ocean of a virgin's womb, a child of divine origin!

In your opinion, why was it necessary for Jesus, the Savior of the world, to be born supernaturally of a virgin?

If that really happened—if the historical Jesus truly was born to a virgin—it would make a compelling case for His deity, wouldn't it? If Jesus was conceived apart from the natural process of conception, we should be satisfied that He pretty much *had* to be God, right? We can see that the Genesis record (3:15) and Isaiah's prophecy (7:14) point to a virgin birth for the Messiah, but is there evidence that what had been promised actually came to pass? Is there any reliable way to investigate the circumstances of Jesus' birth?

Let's begin with the historical record. Seven centuries after Isaiah's prophecy, Matthew reported the extraordinary circumstances of the birth of a child called Jesus of Nazareth. He wrote: "Now this is how Jesus the Messiah was born. His mother, Mary, was engaged to be married to Joseph. But while she was still a virgin, she became pregnant by the Holy Spirit. . . . All of this happened to fulfill the Lord's message through his prophet: 'Look! The virgin will conceive a child! She will give birth to a son, and he will be called Immanuel (meaning, God is with us)'" (Matthew 1:18, 22-23).

The Gospel of Luke, written by the careful historian whose writings have been repeatedly supported by archaeology, records the appearance of the angel Gabriel to Mary and his announcement that she would give birth to the Messiah. Mary answered with a question: "But how can I have a baby? I am a virgin." Gabriel replied, "The Holy Spirit will come upon you, and the power of the Most High will overshadow you. So the baby born to you will be holy, and he will be called the Son of God" (Luke 1:34-35).

Week of AUGUST 8

A Glorious Irony

But among the most significant evidences of Jesus' virgin birth are those contained in the accounts of how the people of Jesus' hometown, Nazareth, reacted to Him after He began His public ministry.

On one occasion, after Jesus had taught in the synagogue, the people He had grown up among said, "'He's just the carpenter, the son of Mary....' They were deeply offended and refused to believe in him" (Mark 6:3). The label "son of Mary" was an unambiguous insult in a society that called children by the name of their fathers—except, of course, in the case of children whose paternity was doubted.

Read John 8:41. What did Jesus' opponents insinuate about Him? _____

What is your personal response to that insult made about Jesus? _____

That insult and the reference to Jesus as the "son of Mary" imply that it was common knowledge in Jesus' hometown that Jesus had been conceived before Mary's wedding to—and without the help of—Joseph.

In other words, it seems very likely that the circumstances of Jesus' miraculous birth—to a virgin—caused Him to be labeled as an illegitimate child in the society of His day. Thus, as a direct result of the unusual circumstances of His birth, He not only accepted the robe of humanity but undoubtedly endured cruel taunts on the playground of His childhood and coarse ridicule from critics as an adult.

In an irony of unbelief, the evidence of His divine glory became a smear on His human reputation! This irony persisted in some of the vehemently anti-Christian writings of Jewish rabbis in the years following His death. The rabbis invented a story that cast Jesus as the illegitimate son of a Roman soldier named Panthera, "unintentionally admitting that Jesus was not born of an ordinary marriage," as the third-century theologian and biblical scholar Origen put it.

> "In an irony of unbelief, the evidence of His divine glory became a smear on His human reputation!"
> —Josh McDowell

The evidence for the Virgin Birth not only points to the conclusion that Jesus of Nazareth is who He claimed to be but also shows how thorough was His identification with us. Though He was God, He humbled Himself and willingly endured the sneers and scorn of His contemporaries in order to be born of a virgin and fulfill His mission as the Messiah, the Son of God, "the visible image of the invisible God" (Colossians 1:15).

Read Philippians 2:6-7 and fill in the blanks.
Jesus was _____, yet He _____ Himself by becoming _____.

How has today's discussion of how Jesus' contemporaries responded to His virgin birth helped you appreciate the truth of Philippians 2:6-7? _____

_____

> "Who, being in very nature God, did not consider equality with God something to be grasped, but made himself nothing, taking the very nature of a servant, being made in human likeness" (Phil. 2:6-7, NIV).

day Five

The Miracles of Christ

The fulfillment of all those messianic prophecies in one person, Jesus Christ, and the miracle of the Virgin Birth ought to fill us—and our children—with awe and wonder. But these are not the only evidences that convince us that the man called Jesus is also the incarnate Son of God.

Read John 5:36 and 10:25,38. What did Jesus point to as evidence that He was God's Son? _____

_____

> "I have testimony weightier than that of John [the Baptist]. For the very work that the Father has given me to finish, and which I am doing, testifies that the Father has sent me" (John 5:36, NIV).

> "The miracles I do in my Father's name speak for me" (John 10:25, NIV).

> "Even though you do not believe me, believe the miracles, that you may know and understand that the Father is in me, and I in the Father" (John 10:38, NIV).

Jesus clearly intended His miracles to be understood as a validation of His deity. As the apostle Peter said on the Day of Pentecost, "Jesus of Nazareth was a man accredited by God to you by miracles, wonders and signs, which God did among you through him" (Acts 2:22, NIV). And the apostle John, pointing to Christ's deity, reports that Jesus did many other "miraculous signs" that weren't even recorded for us (John 20:30).

Week of AUGUST 8

But those recorded miracles are not only sufficient to convince us Jesus was truly who He claimed to be; they ought to impress us with the awesome power and compassion of the Incarnate One, and cause us to exclaim, "A man who could do that is no ordinary man; He had to be God Himself!"

Who else but God has the mastery Jesus demonstrated over the human body, weather, gravity, and even death itself? Who else could

- Calm a storm (see Matthew 8)
- Make a mute person speak (see Matthew 9)
- Feed 5,000 people with five loaves and two fish (see Matthew 14)
- Cast out demons (see Mark 5)
- Walk on water (see Mark 6)
- Bring sight to the blind (see Mark 10)
- Curse a fig tree (see Mark 11)
- Foretell the future (see Mark 14)
- Heal a paralyzed man (see Luke 5)
- Raise a boy from the dead (see Luke 7)
- Heal incurable hemorrhaging (see Luke 8)
- Cleanse lepers (see Luke 17)
- Turn water into wine (see John 2)
- Make the lame walk (see John 5)
- Forgive sin (see John 8)
- Raise a man from the dead (see John 11)

The miracles of Jesus—if we but consider them openly and confront them fairly—ought to do more than convince us that Jesus is who He said He is. His miracles ought to prompt us to wonder, *Who but God can do such things?* They should move us to cry out, like Thomas, "My Lord and my God!" (John 20:28). As Jesus urged His disciples, "Believe that I am in the Father and the Father is in me. Or at least believe because of what you have seen me do" (John 14:11).

The evidences of Christ's deity—the messianic prophecies, His virgin birth, and His many miracles—are recorded so we can believe in Him with deepened conviction, being convinced Jesus Christ is who He said He is.

What miracles have you observed in your own life? What has been your response to those miracles?
❑ Whew—was I lucky!
❑ What an odd coincidence.
❑ "My Lord and my God!"
❑ Other: _____

If you desire to dig deeper . . .

The Gospel of John lists seven of Jesus' works that validated His claim to be from God. Scan the following Scriptures and note the miracles performed by Jesus in each passage.

- John 2:1-11
- John 4:43-54
- John 5:1-15
- John 6:1-13
- John 6:16-21
- John 9:1-6
- John 11:38-44

NOTES

To the Leader:

If you have had new members join in the middle of this study, provide them with a copy of *MasterWork*. Offer to meet with them sometime this week to review what you have studied so far.

Before the Session

1. Enlist five volunteers to read aloud during Step 4: Genesis 21:12; Numbers 24:17; Genesis 49:10; Isaiah 11:1; and Jeremiah 23:5.
2. Read "During the Session." Choose the teaching steps you will use.

During the Session

1. Welcome participants. Open with prayer requests and prayer.
2. Begin the session by telling a few good news/bad news jokes: 1. The preacher announced, "There's bad news—the new roof will cost $50,000. The good news is we've got plenty of money. The bad news is . . . the money is still in your pockets. 2. The slave driver of a Roman galley yelled to the slaves, "I've got good news and bad news. The good news is you'll be getting double rations tonight. The bad news is . . . the commander's son wants to water ski." 3. The plane had been up in the air a while when the captain came on the intercom. "Ladies and gentlemen, I have good news and bad news. The good news is we have a tailwind behind us and we're making good time. The bad news is . . . we're lost."
3. Comment that often times it seems all good news is counteracted by bad news. However, in God's economy, good news is victorious over the bad. Ask someone to read Genesis 3:15. Comment, *From the very instant the bad news of sin entered our world, God announced that good news was coming through the incarnation of His Son.*
4. Ask participants to raise their hands if they skip the long genealogy sections when they read the Bible. Discuss why the genealogies, especially those listed in Matthew 1 and Luke 3, are more than just lists of hard-to-pronounce names. Request the pre-enlisted volunteers read Genesis 21:12; Numbers 27:14; Genesis 49:10; Isaiah 11:1; and Jeremiah 23:5. After each verse, direct learners to state which portion of Luke 3 (in the margin of Day 1) states the fulfillment of that verse.
5. Optional Step: Ask two members to read the dialogue on pages 120-121, ending with "Listen to this. . . ." Use this dialogue to discuss the role of predictive prophecy concerning the coming of the Incarnate One.
6. Ask learners to turn to the list of fulfilled prophecies on pages 121-122. Briefly review these prophecies and Jesus' fulfillment of them.

Week of AUGUST 8

Then say, *"Jesus fulfilled 60 major Old Testament prophecies (with about 270 additional ramifications)—all of which were made more than 400 years before His birth."* Immediately add, *"Further, in just* **one day** *Jesus fulfilled no fewer than 29 specific prophecies spoken at least 500 years earlier about Him!"* Ask: *Have you ever heard this before? How is this possible?*

7. Hold up a quarter and ask, How can you use a coin as a witnessing tool? Guide learners to review McDowell's silver dollar statistical illustration from Day 2. Ask, *What is just as important as convincing someone that Jesus really was God in the flesh?* Remind learners of Dr. McDowell's assertion that the promise of an intimate relationship with God is what will move people beyond belief to convictions.

8. Read Isaiah 7:14. Invite volunteers to share their responses to the activity in Day 3. Request a volunteer read Mark 6:1-3. Ask: *How did this week's lesson cause you to consider the human side of Christ's experience on earth in a new light? How do we treat "God with us" with the same disregard as the persons did from Jesus' hometown?*

9. Read Revelation 5:11-14 and ask learners to compare Jesus' experience on earth with His experience in heaven. Ask, *How does this comparison enhance your appreciation of the Incarnation?*

10. Comment that Matthew and Luke pointed to the virgin birth as evidence Jesus was the incarnate Son of God. Ask, *What evidence of His deity did Jesus point to?* Ask a volunteer to read John 5:36. Ask: *What does the quality of the work you perform tell others about you? What should the works Jesus did tell others about Jesus? Why?* Ask volunteers to state miracles Jesus performed while on earth. [Draw from the list in Day 5, page 129, to supplement responses.] Discuss: *How do these miracles impress you with Jesus' power? How do they impress you with Jesus' compassion?* Allow volunteers to share how they have observed Jesus' power and compassion through His miracles in their own lives.

11. Challenge participants to name specific ways they can speak and behave to demonstrate that their relationship with Jesus, God Incarnate, is real, relevant, and right now. Close in prayer.

After the Session

1. Read next week's lesson and complete the learning activities.
2. Promote your next class fellowship, encouraging regular participants to invite their unchurched friends.

NOTES

Is the Bible Reliable?

When the Book of the Law Was Lost

If the Bible is just a helpful collection of nice thoughts, then it doesn't matter too much if parts have disappeared or been mistranslated over the years. If the Bible is merely another version of truth, then it makes little difference if it is accurate. But if the Bible is God's instruction manual for living, our road map to heaven, and the main means by which we can know God, then it becomes extremely important to know whether it's reliable, whether it was recorded exactly as God gave it, and whether it's been accurately passed down to us. If we truly understand what the Bible is—that is, if we understand how important it is to each of our lives—then questions about its reliability become suddenly and critically important.

So just how reliable is that historical record? What if the people writing the Bible didn't put down everything God said? Or what if they got it all wrong? These questions have already been answered in the Bible itself, in an incident recorded in the Old Testament.

The incident took place in Judah, during a period when a young man named Josiah reigned as king. At that time, the people of Judah had been worshiping idols for many years, and many of the old ways had been neglected or lost. But Josiah "began to seek the God of his ancestor David" (2 Chronicles 34:3). He decreed the destruction of the pagan idols and altars that dotted the land and began an effort to repair, restore, and reconsecrate the temple in Jerusalem.

One day, as Hilkiah the high priest was working amid the flurry of the temple restoration efforts, an ancient scroll was discovered. The priest's hands must have trembled as he rolled through the scroll, reading words that had been lost many years earlier. Recognizing its importance, Hilkiah conveyed the scroll to a man named Shaphan, the king's private secretary.

How would you respond to someone who said, "The Bible is so full of inaccuracies you cannot trust what it says"?

_____

_____

Week of AUGUST 15

As Shaphan read from the scroll to Josiah, the king no doubt recognized the words—even though he had never heard them before—because much of what Shaphan read had been circulated for years by word of mouth, from parent to child and sage to student. Josiah, like Shaphan and Hilkiah, recognized this as "the Book of the Law of the Lord as it had been given through Moses" (2 Chronicles 34:14).

When Josiah heard the words from the scroll, he tore his clothes with his bare hands. "We have not been doing what this scroll says we must do" (2 Chronicles 34:21). He understood that, regardless of his good intentions, God had not been revealed to his people because they had been without the written revelation of God.

The story of King Josiah and his times emphasizes how dangerous it would be if God's Word were lost, distorted, altered, or misrepresented to us through inaccurate copying over hundreds or thousands of years. A distorted revelation produces distorted results.

Similarly, what if, during the copying of Mark's Gospel some hundred years after he wrote it, someone added five chapters? Imagine a person's adding to or twisting around the things Jesus said or did. What if the things Jesus said—the words of eternal life that He spoke—were changed or exaggerated down through the years? If the words God gave to Moses, David, Matthew, and Peter were later changed or carelessly copied, how could we be sure we are coming to know the one true God? How could we be confident that the commands we're obeying are a true reflection of God's nature and character?

If we hope to enjoy the benefits of knowing God, we must be sure that we have a Bible that accurately represents what God inspired people to write on His behalf. If the Word of God was not accurately recorded and relayed to us—then we and our children, like Josiah and the nation of Judah, will be cheated in our efforts to know God and may be exposed to "curses, confusion, and disillusionment" (Deuteronomy 28:20).

> **Check how you'd most likely respond if one day God's Word were lost to you.**
> ❏ I'd never miss it.
> ❏ I'd be puzzled when I couldn't find it in my car on the way to church.
> ❏ It would disturb me at first, but I'd get over it.
> ❏ I would grieve every day because the Bible is a vital part of my daily existence.

The Written Revelation

God has a redemptive, relational purpose in giving us His inspired Word, and He has declared that He will not allow the Bible—the relational revelation of Himself—to be lost, twisted, or distorted. As Jesus said, He will permit nothing to impede His purpose. "Heaven and earth will disappear," Jesus said, "but my words will remain forever" (Matthew 24:35).

God is so passionate about His relationship with us and our kids that He has personally—and miraculously—provided the inspiration of His Word, supervised its transmission, and repeatedly reinforced its reliability so that all those who have open eyes and open hearts may believe it with assurance and conviction.

Nations may have rejected it, tyrants may have tried to stamp it out, heretics may have tried to distort it, but the evidence for the Bible's reliability is sufficient to assure us and our kids that the Bible has remained a true reflection of reality—of who God is—and that "it is stronger and more permanent than heaven and earth" (Luke 16:17). Moreover, an examination of how God has meticulously and miraculously protected the integrity of His Word will impress us and move us with the depth of God's love for us and His faithfulness toward us (see Psalm 36:5).

God spoke, and at His word the universe blazed into being. Then He whose language is heavenly, whose every word is eternal, condescended to express Himself within the crude limitations of human language, like a master architect stacking building blocks on the floor with a child.

That is but one miracle of God's Word, the first of many. He whose words generated light and heat at the creation of the world, spoke through forty ordinary human beings—shepherds, soldiers, prophets, poets, monarchs, scholars, statesmen, musicians, masters, servants, scholars, tax collectors, and tentmakers—to reveal himself to us and our children. But it's not just that He chose human language and human scribes to record His words that should impress us; He also took great care to ensure that those words were recorded exactly as He intended.

Read Matthew 5:18.

Which portion of God's Word will last forever? Check your answer.
- ❏ Only the really important parts about creation and salvation.
- ❏ The teachings of Jesus that tell us how to live a moral life.
- ❏ The great stories that get handed down from one generation to another.
- ❏ Every single detail, from the smallest letter to the least stroke of a pen.

Week of AUGUST 15

You see, many ancient writings adhered only loosely to the facts of the events they reported. Some highly regarded authors of the ancient world, for example, reported events that took place many years before they were born, in countries they had never visited! And while their writing may be largely factual, historians admit that greater credibility must be granted to writers who were both geographically and chronologically close to the events they report.

With that in mind, look at the loving care God took when He inspired the writing of the New Testament, for example! The overwhelming weight of scholarship confirms that the accounts of Jesus' life, the history of the early church, and the letters that form the bulk of the New Testament were all written by men who were either eyewitnesses of the events they recorded or contemporaries of eyewitnesses. He selected Matthew, Mark, and John to write the Gospels. These were men who could say such things as, "This report is from an eyewitness giving an accurate account" (John 19:35). He spoke through Luke the physician to record the third Gospel and the Book of Acts, using as "source material the reports . . . from the early disciples and other eyewitnesses of what God [did] in fulfillment of his promises" (Luke 1:2).

God could have spoken through anyone, from anywhere, to write His words about Christ. But He worked through eyewitnesses such as John, who said, "We are telling you about what we ourselves have actually seen and heard" (1 John 1:3). He worked through Peter, who stated, "For we did not follow cunningly devised fables when we made known to you the power and coming of our Lord Jesus Christ, but were eyewitnesses of His majesty" (2 Peter 1:16, NKJV). And whom did He choose as His most prolific writer? The apostle Paul, whose dramatic conversion from persecutor of Christians to planter of churches made him perhaps the most credible witness of all!

God didn't stop there. He also transmitted His inspired Word through His apostles to appeal to the firsthand knowledge of their contemporaries, even their most severe opponents (see Acts 2:32; 3:15; 13:31; 1 Corinthians 15:3-8). They not only said, "Look, we saw this," or "We heard that," but they were also so confident as to say in effect, "Check it out," "Ask around," and "You know it as well as I do!" Such challenges demonstrate a supreme confidence that the "God-breathed" Word was recorded exactly as God spoke it to them (2 Timothy 3:16, NIV).

Read Luke 1:1-4.

Imagine you were interviewing Dr. Luke, writer of the books of Luke and Acts. Write his answers to your questions below:

Q: Why did you write the book we know as the gospel of Luke?
A: _____
_____

Q: What was the source of your material?
A: _____
_____

Q: How can you be confident everything you recorded is true?
A: _____
_____

Such careful inspiration and supervision of the Bible underlines God's loving purpose, that not a single piece of this relational revelation of Himself be left to chance or recorded incorrectly, so as to deprive us of His protection and provision. Ample evidence exists to suggest that God was very selective in the people He chose to record His words—people who for the most part had firsthand knowledge of key events and who were credible channels to record exactly those truths He wanted us to know.

God's Word Has Been Copied Accurately

It's not difficult to see the superintending work of God in the composition of the Old and New Testaments alike. But still, only the original manuscripts—called autographs—were inspired by God, and none of those is in existence today. What we read now are printed copies based on ancient handwritten copies of yet other copies of the original.

The Bible was composed and transmitted in an era before printing presses. If a document was to be preserved and passed down to the next generation, the manuscript had to be written by hand. Over time, the ink would fade, and the material it was written on would deteriorate, so new copies would have to be hand copied or the document would be lost forever.

But doesn't the making of hand-copied reproductions open up the whole process to error? After all, who's to say that a copier didn't omit some of God's words? What if years later someone who was not inspired by God decided to add some new idea to the Bible? How do we know that a weary copier, blurry-eyed from lack of sleep, didn't skip whole sections or misquote some key verses? What if it's true that the Bible is a collection of outdated writings that are riddled with inaccuracies and distortions?

Even if the Bible's human authors recorded exactly what God inspired them to write, how can we believe that what we read today is what they originally wrote? How can we be sure that the manuscripts available to us today are an accurate transmission of the originals?

Week of AUGUST 15

God has not left us to wonder. Just as He went to great lengths to ensure that His Word was recorded exactly, so He miraculously supervised its transmission to ensure that His Word was also relayed accurately from one generation to another.

One of the ways God ensured that His Word was relayed accurately was by choosing, calling, and cultivating a nation of men and women who took the Book of the Law very seriously. God commanded and instilled in the Jewish people a great reverence for His Word. Read in the margin what God told them from their first days as a nation in Deuteronomy 6:3,6-9.

Do these verses describe your regard for the Bible?
❏ Yes ❏ No
Does your attitude towards God's Word make you a trustworthy candidate to pass down God's Word to the next generation?
❏ Yes ❏ No
If you answered Yes, explain why. _____
If you answered No, what will you change this week so you can accurately relay God's Word to your world?

_____

"Listen closely, Israel, to everything I say. . . . Commit yourselves wholeheartedly to these commands I am giving you today. Repeat them again and again to your children. Talk about them when you are at home and when you are away on a journey, when you are lying down and when you are getting up again. Tie them to your hands as a reminder, and wear them on your forehead. Write them on the doorposts of your house and on your gates" (Deut. 6:3,6-9).

That attitude toward the commands of God became such a part of the Jewish identity that a class of Jewish scholars called the Sopherim, from a Hebrew word meaning "scribes," arose between the fifth and third centuries B.C. These custodians of the Hebrew Scriptures dedicated themselves to carefully preserving the ancient manuscripts and producing new copies when necessary.

The Sopherim were eclipsed by the Talmudic scribes, who guarded, interpreted, and commented on the sacred texts from A.D. 100–500. In turn, the Talmudic scribes were followed by the better-known Masoretic scribes (A.D. 500–900).

The zeal of the Masoretes surpassed that of even their most dedicated predecessors. They established detailed and stringent disciplines for copying a manuscript. Their rules were so rigorous that when a new copy was complete, they would give the reproduction equal authority to that of its parent copy because they were thoroughly convinced that they had an exact duplicate.

The Meticulous Scribes

In the providence of God, meticulous scribes were chosen to preserve the Old Testament text for centuries. A scribe would begin his day of transcribing by ceremonially washing his entire body. He would then garb himself in full Jewish dress before sitting at his desk. As he wrote, if he came to the Hebrew name of God, he could not begin writing the name with a quill newly dipped in ink for fear it would smear the page. Once he began writing the name of God, he could not stop or allow himself to be distracted; even if a king was to enter the room, the scribe was obligated to continue without interruption until he finished penning the holy name of the one true God.

The Masoretic guidelines for copying manuscripts also required the following:

- The scroll must be written on the skin of a clean animal.
- Each skin must contain a specified number of columns, equal throughout the entire book.
- The length of each column must extend no less than forty-eight lines or more than sixty lines.
- The column breadth must consist of exactly thirty letters.
- The space of a thread must appear between every consonant.
- The breadth of nine consonants had to be inserted between each section.
- A space of three lines had to appear between each book.
- The fifth book of Moses (Deuteronomy) had to conclude exactly with a full line.
- Nothing—not even the shortest word—could be copied from memory; it had to be copied letter by letter.
- The scribe must count the number of times each letter of the alphabet occurred in each book and compare it to the original.
- If a manuscript was found to contain even one mistake, it was discarded.

How did the careful work of the Masoretic scribes insure that God's Word was accurately copied and passed down over hundreds of years?

_____

_____

Pause and thank God for these ancient meticulous copyists of His Word.

Week of AUGUST 15

What do you think most people today would say about the Masoretes' painstaking attention to detail?
- ☐ They would laugh and call them fools.
- ☐ They would suggest intense therapy for obsessive-compulsive disorder.
- ☐ They would be impressed with the Masoretes but thankful they weren't one of them.
- ☐ They would be thankful the Masoretes were faithful servants and accurately preserved God's Word.

God instilled in the Masoretes such a painstaking reverence for the Hebrew Scriptures to ensure the amazingly accurate transmission of the Book of the Law so that you and I—and our children—would have an accurate revelation of God.

Until recently, however, we had no way of knowing just how amazing the preservation of the Old Testament has been. Before 1947, the oldest complete Hebrew manuscript dated to A.D. 900. But with the discovery of 223 manuscripts in caves on the west side of the Dead Sea, we now have Old Testament manuscripts that have been dated by paleographers at around 125 B.C. These Dead Sea Scrolls, as they are called, are a thousand years older than any previously known manuscripts.

But here's the exciting part: Once the Dead Sea Scrolls were translated and compared with modern versions, the Hebrew Bible proved to be identical, word for word, in more than 95 percent of the text. (The variation of 5 percent consisted mainly of spelling variations. For example, of the 166 words in Isaiah 53, only 17 letters were in question. Of those, 10 letters were a matter of spelling, and 4 were stylistic changes; the remaining 3 letters comprised the word "light," which was added in verse 11.)

In other words, the greatest manuscript discovery of all time revealed that a thousand years of copying the Old Testament produced only excruciatingly minor variations, none of which altered the clear meaning of the text or brought the manuscript's fundamental integrity into question.

The critics will make their pronouncements in opposition to the evidence. However, the overwhelming weight of evidence affirms that God has preserved His Word and accurately relayed it through the centuries so that when you pick up an Old Testament today, you can be utterly confident that you are holding a well-preserved, fully reliable document.

How did the Dead Sea Scrolls prove that God's Word was accurately copied and preserved over hundreds of years?

_____

_____

The New Testament Text

Historians evaluate the textual reliability of ancient literature according to two standards: (1) what the time interval is between the original and the earliest copy; and (2) how many manuscripts are available.

So, for example, virtually everything we know today about Julius Caesar's exploits in the Gallic Wars is derived from ten manuscript copies, the earliest of which dates to within 1,000 years of the time *The Gallic Wars* was written. Our modern text of Livy's *History of Rome* relies on one partial manuscript and nineteen much later copies that are dated from 400 to 1,000 years *after* the original writing. By comparison, the text of Homer's *Iliad* is much more reliable. It is supported by 643 manuscript copies in existence today, with a mere 400-year time gap between the date of composition and the earliest copies we have available for examination today.

But the textual evidence for these classical writers pale in comparison to what God performed in the case of the New Testament text.

Using the accepted standard for evaluating the textual reliability of ancient texts, the New Testament stands alone. It has no equal. No other book of the ancient world can even approach its reliability.

Nearly *25,000* manuscripts of the New Testament repose in the libraries and universities of the world. The earliest of these is a fragment of John's Gospel currently located in the John Rylands Library of Manchester, England; it has been dated to within *50 years* of the date when the apostle John penned the original!

EXTERNAL CONFIRMATION OF GOD'S WORD

God did not stop working when He compiled the massive textual evidence for the reliability of His Word; He has since worked to reinforce the evidence through external means.

A routine criterion in examining the reliability of an historical document is whether *other* historical material confirms or denies the internal testimony of the document itself. Historians ask, "What sources, apart from the literature under examination, substantiate its accuracy and reliability?"

How does the "weight" of biblical manuscripts compare to that of other ancient documents?

Why is this important?

Hold your Bible in your hands. How do you feel when you realize you are holding the very words of God transmitted accurately over thousands of years? Write your thoughts here.

Week of AUGUST 15

In all of history, the Bible is by far the most widely referenced and quoted book. For example, the New Testament alone is so extensively quoted in the ancient manuscripts of nonbiblical authors that all twenty-seven books from Matthew through Revelation could be reconstructed virtually word for word from those sources.

The writings of early Christians like Eusebius (A.D. 339) in his *Ecclesiastical History* and Irenaeus (A.D. 180) in his *Against Heresies* reinforce the text of the apostle John's writings. Clement of Rome (A.D. 95), Ignatius (A.D. 70–110), Polycarp (A.D. 70–156), and Titian (A.D. 170) offer external confirmation of other New Testament accounts. Non-Christian historians such as the first-century Roman historian Tacitus (A.D. 55–117) and the Jewish historian Josephus (A.D. 37–100) confirm the substance of some scriptural accounts. These and other outside sources substantiate the accuracy of the biblical record like that of no other book in history.

However, ancient literature's extrabiblical references are not the only external evidences that support the Bible's reliability. The very stones cry out that God's Word is true. Over and over again through the centuries, the reliability of the Bible has been regularly and consistently supported by archaeology.

It is overwhelming to realize that the God of the universe has superintended the writing and passing down of His words from generation to generation so that you and I can have an accurate revelation of Him. It is truly amazing to hold in your hand a book you can confidently believe is an accurate transmission of God-breathed (inspired) words. And it is thrilling to know that God gives us His Word so that by following His ways we can count on His protection and provision.

But still more astonishing is the fact that the Word of God also reveals our true purpose in life. All of us, and our kids as well, long to know our purpose for living. Whether consciously or subconsciously, we want the answer to the question, "Why am I here?" God's Word provides that answer. In the next lesson, we are going to discover how our young people's convictions about Christ and God's Word can lead them to live the joyous and blessed—and purpose-filled—life they were meant to live.

> To learn more about archaeological confirmation of the Bible, purchase (and read) a copy of Josh McDowell's book *The New Evidence That Demands a Verdict* from your local LifeWay Christian Store.

What is the most amazing fact you discovered in your study this week? _____

Why does it amaze you? _____

Amy SUMMERS

NOTES

To the Leader:

"Take to heart all the words I have solemnly declared to you this day, so that you may command your children to obey carefully all the words of this law. They are not just idle words for you—they are your life" (Deut. 32:46-47).

How do you demonstrate to your class that God's Word is your life? Do you study it like it's your life? Do you obey it like it's your life? Do you present it to your class like it's your life?

Thank God for the privilege of having and teaching His Word of life.

Before the Session

1. Gather a variety of books, such as novels, dictionaries, encyclopedias, auto repair books, travel guides, and so forth.
2. Read "During the Session." Choose the teaching steps you will use.

During the Session

1. Welcome participants. Open with prayer requests and prayer.
2. Display the books. Ask: *Which of these books are you certain contain true information? Which of these books do you depend on to be accurate? Why?* Hold your Bible in one hand and a dictionary in the other. Ask: *If you were to carry these two books down our town's sidewalks and ask passersby which book they believe contains reliable, accurate information, which do you think they would choose? What kind of response do you think you'd get if you performed the same survey in our church hallways? Why is it absolutely essential to be able to trust the Bible as completely true and reliable?* Discuss the "If . . . then" statements in the first paragraph under Day 1.
3. Ask how participants benefit from the books you displayed. Request a volunteer read Psalm 19:7-11 and direct adults to call out the benefits of God's Word. Write responses on the board in one column. Ask adults to name the opposite of each benefit. Write responses in a second column. Challenge adults to silently review each column and determine which more closely resembles their lives. Ask, *If we are not enjoying the benefits of God's Word, what should that tell us?* Comment that it may mean that we, like the Hebrew people in Josiah's day, have lost God's Word.
4. Ask a volunteer to read 2 Chronicles 34:1-4. Ask: *What was the first thing Josiah did when he began to seek the Lord? What must we destroy in our lives if we are seeking God?* Ask someone to read 2 Chronicles 34:8. Ask, *What was Josiah's next step in seeking God?* Comment that it is not enough to destroy sinful practices in our life; we must also strive to rebuild our relationship with God.
5. Request adults read silently 2 Chronicles 34:14-15 and state what was found during the rebuilding of the Temple. Ask: *How could they*

Week of AUGUST 15

lose God's Word—literally forget all about it? How do we forget all about God's Word even when we have several copies in our homes? As you read 2 Chronicles 34:27,31 direct adults to listen for how they should respond when they realize they have neglected God's Word. Call for responses.

6. Ask participants to describe a time they were misquoted or misunderstood because someone added to or deleted from something they had said. Ask why God wrote the Bible. Inquire: *If we get upset when someone alters what we have said, how do you think God feels about someone changing the Words He desires to bring us into relationship with Him?* Ask a volunteer to read Revelation 22:18-19.

7. Discuss the methods God used to insure His Word was written exactly as He wanted and preserved accurately through history. [Eyewitness accounts, inspiration of the Holy Spirit, supervision of its transmission]

8. Ask adults if they've ever been in a completely dark environment and have sensed the presence of another person. Ask: *What alerted you to the fact someone was there?* Agree that breath alerts us to someone's presence. Request a volunteer read 2 Timothy 3:16. Ask: *What does the term "God-breathed" mean to you in relation to the inspiration of Scripture?*

9. Request adults get into pairs and review the information about biblical transmission in Days 3-5, or give a mini-lecture on this material, specifically calling attention to the information on pages 138-140. Then direct them to role-play giving a loving defense of the accuracy of Scripture to a doubting person.

10. Comment that the Bible also has repeatedly been shown to be accurate by external confirmation. Discuss the importance of extrabiblical testimony and archaeology in substantiating the accuracy and reliability of the Bible (Day 5). Discuss the final activity of Day 5.

11. Close in prayer that the adults in your class will be people who believe, read, study, treasure, and live by God's Word.

NOTES

After the Session
1. Read next week's lesson and complete the learning activities.
2. Secure a copy of Josh McDowell's book *The New Evidence That Demands a Verdict* and make it available to interested learners.

The Meaning of God's Word to Our Lives

Does *Reliable* Mean It's True for Everyone?

"There should be enough here to convince just about anybody that the Bible is the most reliable document ever written."

"What have you got?" Duane asked. He pulled his chair beside Allen's to look at the research he had gathered. Lauren, Megan, and Liz also leaned forward as Allen started to lift pages from the stack and pass them around as he explained what he had discovered.

More than an hour later, Lauren leaned back in her chair. "Wow," she said. "I had no idea."

"You've done some excellent work, Allen," Duane said.

Allen leaned back, smiling, clearly pleased.

"Yeah," Lauren said. "It's pretty . . . amazing."

Liz looked at Lauren. "What's wrong, Lauren?" she asked. "You sound like something's still bothering you."

Lauren cocked her head. "I don't know," she said slowly. "I mean, I can see that the Bible's really reliable." She paused. "But there's something about all this that doesn't feel right."

"What do you mean by 'doesn't feel right'?" Liz asked.

"We-e-ll," Lauren said, drawing the word out slowly. "I mean, I can see that the Bible's really reliable." She paused. "But it almost sounds like you're saying that the Bible is true . . . for everyone."

"Yeah," Duane said, "we are saying that."

Lauren blinked a few times. "Oh," she said softly.

"You sound disappointed," Liz suggested.

"Well, yeah," Lauren replied. "It just sounds so . . . exclusive. Because

Week of AUGUST 22

if it's true for everyone, then you're pretty much saying that Jesus is the only way for the whole world . . . and, for some reason, that just doesn't feel right."

Read Acts 4:12. What do you think Lauren would say about Peter's declaration? (Check all that apply)
- ❏ It just doesn't feel right.
- ❏ That's really narrow-minded
- ❏ I'm so thankful I've received salvation through Christ.
- ❏ I've got to make sure others hear about salvation through Christ.

"There is salvation in no one else! There is no other name in all of heaven for people to call on to save them" (Acts 4:12, NLT).

Is your response to Acts 4:12 similar to or different than Lauren's? Circle your answer.

AN EXCLUSIVE BOOK PROCLAIMING AN EXCLUSIVE TRUTH

Lauren is like the majority of our young people. Many of them have been conditioned to believe that their beliefs are very personal and subjective. Remember that while most of our kids (61 percent) believe the Bible provides "a clear and totally accurate description of moral truth," they don't believe that means the Bible is authoritatively true for everyone. The vast majority—81 percent of our youth—claims that "all truth is relative to the individual and his/her circumstance."

Therefore, having been taught that it's up to them to *create* their own truth, to decide whatever is true *for them*, they're uncomfortable with any suggestion that a particular viewpoint is true for everyone. Such a conclusion "feels" too exclusive to them.

With such a mind-set, most of our kids view the Bible *not* as a universally true revelation of the one true God but as a mere resource, a set of inspirational stories and helpful insights that might offer guidance in creating their own "truth."

In your opinion, what is the danger in using the Bible to create your own version of truth? _____

_____

But the Bible isn't a mere resource, a set of inspirational stories and helpful guidelines from which we can form "our own truth," as so many of our kids believe. It is the means by which the one true God has chosen to reveal details of Himself to you and me. When young people encounter the historical accuracy of the Bible, they inevitably come face-to-face with the claims of Christ. That is when our young people, like Lauren, are faced with an inescapable conclusion: Scripture accurately reveals Jesus Christ as the only way to the one true God. And that, of course, flies in the face of their cultural conditioning.

When you hold a Bible in your hand, you are cradling a holy book to be reverenced and hungered after because its very words reveal the God who gives your life its true purpose.

Read 1 Thessalonians 2:13. List the truths this verse declares about the Bible. _____

_____

"And we also thank God continually because, when you received the word of God, which you heard from us, you accepted it not as the word of men, but as it actually is, the word of God, which is at work in you who believe" (1 Thess. 2:13, NIV).

Why Am I Here?

Picture the Hebrew scribe—one of the Sopherim, the ancients who copied and preserved the sacred writings of the Jews—as he enters his small workroom. Since the fall of Jerusalem and the destruction of the temple by the Babylonians in 586 B.C., the Book of the Law was all the Jews had left, their only connection with the God of Abraham, Isaac, and Jacob. The Torah scrolls the scribe kept in clay jars in his workroom contained the very words God gave to Moses and the prophets, and told of God's passion for relationship with them (see Exodus 34:14). Those words written on animal skins revealed the universal dilemma shared by the whole human race, the sin that separated them from God, and His merciful intention to solve that dilemma. Those stylus marks detailed God's special relationship with His chosen people and told of His promise to lead them back to Him—a promise that included restoring them again as a nation in relationship with Him as their king and loving Lord, where all things would one day be as they were in the pristine Garden of Eden.

Therefore, this scribe—like *all* the Sopherim—treated those words, those books, with the utmost care and attention. He washed ceremonial-

Week of AUGUST 22

ly, meticulously, before picking up a stylus. He copied every word, every letter, with painstaking care. And, lest anyone misunderstand what God had said through his misreading or miscopying of a fading, crumbling, or stained scroll, he carefully buried those that were old or marred. He did all these things (and more) because he believed an awesome, universal truth, one that had been proclaimed by God to Hosea: "I don't want your sacrifices," he said, *"I want you to know God"* (Hosea 6:6, emphasis added).

Yahweh, the almighty God of the universe, has revealed Himself in human language so that we will come to know Him intimately—so intimately, in fact, that we become like Him. And that awesome, universal truth answers our pressing question "Why are we here?"

> "God knew his people in advance, and he chose them to become like his Son" (Rom. 8:29, NLT).

Read Romans 8:29 and 2 Corinthians 3:18. Why were you put on this earth, according to these two verses?

_____

> "We, who with unveiled faces all reflect the Lord's glory, are being transformed into his likeness with ever-increasing glory, which comes from the Lord, who is the Spirit" (2 Cor. 3:18, NIV).

Our purpose in life—your purpose and your children's purpose—is to know God and become more and more like Him.

When we become more and more like God, we glorify Him because we reflect positively on Him—on His character and nature. We also gratify Him because seeing us reflect His nature gives Him great pleasure. The apostle Paul said, "Long ago, even before he made the world, God loved us and chose us in Christ to be holy and without fault in his eyes. His unchanging plan has always been to adopt us into his own family by bringing us to himself through Jesus Christ. And this gave him great pleasure" (Ephesians 1:4-5).

> "Seeing us reflect His nature gives Him great pleasure."
> —Josh McDowell

Just as a human father swells with pride when his child follows in his footsteps and just as a human mother takes pleasure in her youngster living out the values she's instilled, so our heavenly Father exults to see us become more and more like Him.

Do you more often:
- ❑ offer a sacrifice to God in an attempt to please Him?
- ❑ seek to become like God by getting to know Him through His Word?

The Written Revelation

God's taking on human form through the Incarnation reveals God's relational heart, which says to each of us, "I want a relationship with you. And in that relationship I want you to know me and be like me." Yet it is the written revelation of Himself in His Word that gives us a description of His image. God's written Word is the picture-perfect lens of His image. It is as if God is saying to you and me and our children, "I have preserved for you my written Word, as a perfect lens to see me for who I am. Read its pages to know me, so you can reflect what you see of me. Become intimate with me and through our close relationship together you will enjoy the true meaning in living, for you will bear the fruit of my nature—love, joy, peace, patience, kindness, goodness, faithfulness, gentleness and self-control" (see Galatians 5:22-23).

> **Describe the pictures of God you see in the following passages:**
> Isaiah 31:4-5 _____
> Isaiah 40:11 _____
> Isaiah 49:15-16 _____

"Whatever is good and perfect comes to us from God above" (Jas. 1:17, NLT).

When you and I and our children begin to fulfill our purpose (of knowing God and becoming more and more like Him), we begin to live out the truly meaningful life that God originally designed for us. God created us in His likeness and image so that we could relate to Him and enjoy all the blessings that come from being godly. Acting according to God's ways brings blessing because all that is defined as perfectly right and good is derived from His nature (see James 1:17).

We were created to live happy, fulfilled lives. We were made to know the gratifying joy of being accepted, approved of, and appreciated, with the ability to freely love and be loved. We were designed to experience a fulfillment and satisfaction beyond measure, a contentment and peace

Week of AUGUST 22

beyond understanding, and an abundant life beyond belief. And that kind of meaningful life comes only from living in fellowship with God and conforming to His likeness. Sin all but destroyed God's design, but because of Christ we can now be adopted into God's family and begin the transformation process, allowing the divine nature of God to permeate our lives. And without God's Word, we would be without the handbook on living an abundant life, we would be without direction, and most important, we would be without an accurate revelation of God, unable to know Him for who He is. That is the significance of the Bible to each one of us and to our everyday lives. God's Word is the perfect lens to see—and then reflect—the divine nature of God.

On the scale below, mark with an "S" how clearly you see God's nature in His Word. Mark with an "R" how clearly you reflect God's nature to others.

|—————|—————|—————|—————|—————|

Not at all   **It's fuzzy**   **Very clear**

What changes will you make so you can see and reflect God more clearly?

_____

Empowered by the Spirit and the Word

God has revealed Himself to us in written form. But He has done more.

Read the verses from John 14 and 1 Corinthians 2 in the margin and answer the following.

Who has God given believers? _____

What does this Person do with God's Word? _____

_____

"And I will ask the Father, and he will give you another Counselor, who will never leave you. He is the Holy Spirit, who leads into all truth. . . . He will teach you everything and will remind you of everything I myself have told you" (John 14:16-17,26, NLT).

"No one can know God's thoughts except God's own Spirit. And God has actually given us his Spirit . . . so we can know the wonderful things God has freely given us. . . . We speak words given to us by the Spirit, using the Spirit's words to explain spiritual truths. . . . We who have the Spirit understand these things" (1 Cor. 2:11-15, NLT).

- "His patience will replace your impatience."
- "His peace will replace your anxiety."
- "His love will replace your self-centeredness."
- "His life will become your life."

Have those statements become a reality in your life?
❏ Yes ❏ No

But if we don't hide the words of God away in our hearts, how can His Spirit remind us of what Christ said? If we don't learn what God is like through His picture-perfect Word, then how can we cooperate with the Spirit as He replicates that image in our lives?

Jesus wants *you* to know *him* intimately, so intimately that His patience will replace your impatience, His peace will replace your anxiety, His love will replace your self-centeredness—His life will become your life. He longs to become "more and more at home in your [heart] as you trust in him" (Ephesians 3:17). But in order for that to happen, you must first know Him through the picture-perfect lens of His Word and then allow Him to live His life in and through you. "He died for everyone so that those who receive his new life will no longer live to please themselves. Instead, they will live to please Christ" (2 Corinthians 5:15).

God doesn't want you to go to His Word to simply learn the rules of the Christian life. He doesn't want you to read the Bible only to gain inspiration to live better. He wants you to see His Word as an open door to His heart, a way to know Him for who He is. And His invitation to know Him brings with it the power for Him to live His life through you.

Look up and read 2 Peter 1:3-4 in your Bible and fill in the blanks to complete the sentence.
K_____ God provides us with p_____ to live a g_____ life so we can e_____ the corruption of this world and s_____ in God's divine n_____.

That is what we want for our young people, isn't it? And all that is possible as you and I—and our young people—come to know Christ better by making the reliable Word a centerpiece of our lives. Not by using the Scripture as a "suggestion manual" or self-help book to create our own brand of truth. Not even by trying to obey a set of rules or trying to live a good life. Intimacy with God and living like Christ happens supernaturally as we gain a clear, true vision of God and His ways, make His Son at home in our hearts, and thus receive "his divine power [that] gives us everything we need for living a godly life" (2 Peter 1:3-4).

Week of AUGUST 22

Living What We Believe

None of us is angelic yet. But we can become more and more like Christ. Look at what the apostle Paul said in Philippians 3:12: "I don't mean to say that I have already achieved these things, or that I have already reached perfection! But I keep working toward that day when I will finally be all that Christ Jesus saved me for and wants me to be."

You see, as the Holy Spirit shows us in His Word what Jesus is like, He leads us into a deeper love relationship with Him and a process of being made more and more like Him. We "are being transformed into his likeness with ever-increasing glory," Paul says in 2 Corinthians 3:18. In fact, before Paul told the Philippians that he wasn't angelic yet, he began his letter to them by saying, "'I am sure that God, who began the good work within you, will continue his work until it is finally finished on that day when Christ Jesus comes back again'" (Philippians 1:6). It's a process. A process that God will keep doing in you until Christ returns.

One of the first steps in this process is to get to know God's Word so you will fall in love with the God of the Word. Knowing His Word can help us keep from many failings.

> **Read what David said in Psalm 119:4-11 and answer the following:**
> **What must you do with God's Word?** _____
>
> **What can knowing God's Word do for you?** _____
>
> _____

A WORD OF CAUTION AND SOME IMPORTANT GUIDELINES
We can be confident that when we read the Bible, we are getting a reliable revelation of God. It is a perfect lens that allows us to see God for who He is and His ways for what they are. But does that mean if our young people go to the Bible to know Jesus better, we can be confident they will come away with a correct understanding of God and how to follow His

ways? If the Holy Spirit is there to guide them into all truth, they can't go wrong—right?

Well, not exactly. A note of caution is in order.

Our adversary, the devil, may not be able to destroy the Word of God, but he still works to twist and abuse Scripture as he did when he tempted Christ in the wilderness (see Isaiah 40:8; Matthew 4:1-11; 5:18). He cannot change the words already written down in Scripture, but he still tries hard to cloud our minds and hearts, and cause us to ignore, misunderstand, or misinterpret God's Word. He cannot change the reliability of the Bible, but if he can prompt its disuse or misuse, he can still achieve many of his deceptive ends.

Compare Genesis 2:16-17 with Genesis 3:1-3. How did Satan twist God's words? _____

What evidence do you see that Satan led Eve to misinterpret God's command?_____

That is why we need clear guidelines for interpreting and applying what the Bible says, guidelines that will ensure that the image we see reflected in the pages of Scripture is an accurate image of the God who wants us to know Him.

Here are three fundamental guidelines for interpreting the Bible.

1. Ask "What Does It Say?" We do this by running Scripture through a six-part grid represented by these questions: Who? What? When? Where? Why? and How? We may not be able to answer all six questions in every passage, but by asking and answering as many as possible, we will come to understand what the Word of God is saying to us.

2. Ask "What Does It Mean?" Understanding the significance of a portion of Scripture *is not* the same as asking, "What does it *mean to me or you?*" The words of the Bible have an objective meaning of their own—the meaning God intended. When we read a passage of the Bible, we need to ask, "What is the objective meaning or significance of this passage?" and then let the Scripture interpret that for us. This is where Bible study tools (such as concordances, study Bibles, Bible commentaries in which you can read what scholars have written about the passage, Bible encyclopedias, Bible dictionaries, Bible atlases, cross-references, other Bible translations and paraphrases) and techniques (such as studying the context, studying the words and phrases) are helpful.

Week of AUGUST 22

3. Ask "How Does It Apply?" We need to experience the objective meaning of God's Word in our own lives and relationships. At least three categories of questions can help us to experience the truth of God's Word in our lives: *(a) identify how the truth relates to your life; (b) identify the hindrances to putting the truth into practice in your life and what you will do about them; (c) commit to experiencing the truth by identifying what practical steps you can take to make the truth of Scripture an experienced reality in your life.*

Again, it's important to emphasize the goal of reading and studying the Bible. We shouldn't study the Bible simply to know what Scripture says. We should read God's words for a relational purpose—to know God, to understand His ways, and to allow Him to live His life in and through our lives.

> **Apply these three guidelines on pages 152-153 to a study of Psalm 91:1-16. On a separate sheet of paper, answer as many of the six questions in Guideline 1 as possible. If at all possible, consult Bible study tools to gain further insight into the meaning of this passage. Then write your responses to the three categories of questions described in Guideline 3.**

leader Guide

NOTES

To the Leader:

What does the atmosphere of your class say to a visitor? Prepare the physical environment of your room, and more importantly, the welcoming attitude of yourself and your members so when each person arrives they get the message, "We want to have a relationship with you; we accept you without condition; we want to understand you."

Before the Session

1. Read "During the Session." Choose the teaching steps you will use.
2. Enlist two volunteers to read Exodus 34:5-7 and Nehemiah 8:10 in Step 7.
3. Complete the activity at the end of Day 5 on page 153 by doing a personal study of Psalm 91, consulting commentaries and other Bible study tools.

During the Session

1. Welcome participants. Open with prayer requests and prayer.
2. Request those present for last week's session to share what fascinated them about how God has preserved His Word. Ask how that study helped them have more confidence in the reliability of the Bible. Ask: *Just because it's reliable and true for you, does that mean it's true for everyone? Explain why this is an important issue for today.*
3. Invite a volunteer to read 2 Timothy 2:15. Discuss these questions: *What are we to do with God's Word? What are correct and incorrect ways to handle the word of truth? What is the danger of using the Bible to create your own version of truth?*
4. Request someone read 1 Thessalonians 2:13. Allow volunteers to share what they learned about the Bible from this verse (last activity of Day 1). Ask a volunteer to read Hebrews 4:12. Ask: *What makes God's words recorded in the Bible different from other printed inspiring words? How are God's words living—is it some sort of magic?* Lead adults to understand God's Word is living because the Bible is an actual revelation of God Himself.
5. Ask: *Why did God reveal Himself through human language?* [So we could come to know Him intimately.] *What happens when you get to know someone intimately?* Invite adults to share instances of a husband and wife acting alike or of children imitating a parent. Ask: *What happens when you get to know God intimately through the study of His Word?* [You become more like Him.] *How does that enable us to fulfill the purpose for which we've been put on earth?* Ask volunteers to read Romans 8:29 and 2 Corinthians 3:18. Inquire

Week of AUGUST 22

whether adults were surprised to discover their purpose in life is to become like Christ, and if so, why.

6. Ask someone to read the quotation in the margin of Day 2. Ask those adults who are parents to share times they have enjoyed seeing their children imitate them and instances when they have cringed to see themselves reflected in their children. Ask, *Why would God receive only pleasure in seeing us reflect His nature?* [Because His nature is all good.] Read James 1:17 in the margin of Day 3.

7. Ask someone to recall the fruit of God's nature listed in Galatians 5:22-23 (Day 3). Write the fruit on the board. Allow volunteers to share pictures of God they saw in the passages from Isaiah in the exercise under Day 3. Ask them to indicate the fruit of God's nature each passage reflects. Check each fruit on the board as it is mentioned. Request the two pre-enlisted volunteers read Exodus 34:6-7a and Nehemiah 8:10. Again ask the class to indicate the fruit of God's nature reflected in those passages and check the fruits mentioned.

8. Request the class turn to Isaiah 48:17-18 and follow along as you read. Ask, *What is the relationship between God's Word and a peaceful, abundant life?* Request two volunteers read aloud the passages about the Holy Spirit in the margin of Day 4, page 149. Inquire, *What is the relationship between God's Word and the Holy Spirit?* Read aloud the two rhetorical questions following the first activity of Day 4. Ask, *What should we be doing with God's Word?*

9. Ask the class to recall Dr. McDowell's caution issued under Day 5 about using and interpreting the Bible. Ask the class to turn in their Bibles to Psalm 91. Request someone read verses 11-12. Then read aloud Matthew 4:5-7 and ask how Satan twisted God's words from Psalm 91. Explain that the best way to know if Satan is misusing God's Word is to know God's Word. Study Psalm 91, using the "What Does It Say? What Does It Mean? How Does It Apply?" guidelines from Day 5. Encourage learners to share insights from their personal study. Share helpful information you gained from your commentary study.

10. Close in prayer.

After the Session

1. Read next week's lesson and complete the learning activities.

Because He Lives

In a Life Where Death Reigns

What is there to say to people facing tragedy? It's true that having strong convictions about Christ and His Word does lead us to trust in Him as our Savior, Comforter, and Power Source. It does help us to enjoy a closer relationship with our loving Father God. But there's more.

We must also gain a deepened conviction about Christ's resurrection and an understanding of what His resurrection means to each of us personally. Without such a conviction, it's extremely easy to lose our perspective, especially when tragedy strikes and life seems to make no sense. The meaning of the resurrection of Jesus Christ enables us to answer a third crucial question: Where am I going? And that gives our identity and purpose a clear and proper perspective.

The resurrection of Jesus Christ and its relational meaning to us completes the picture of reality. It allows us to see life with all its struggles from God's perspective. A deepened conviction in Christ's resurrection can equip us to face whatever happens in life—good or bad—with gratitude, courage, and optimism. It's what our children need, particularly with all the challenges they face in their daily lives today. It's what all of us need.

The disruption and decay of this earth and the inevitability of death are a living reality. Pain and loss are felt every minute of every day somewhere in the world. As often as life serves up pain and heartache, we are rarely willing to accept it. Something inside us says, "This makes no sense," and we hope that life will be better tomorrow. But even if tomorrow is better, it won't mean much eventually because some day, all that we have and hold will fade from our grasp, and we will die.

How do you feel about the difficulties in this life? Circle the word(s) that best complete this statement— I most often respond to the unfairness of this world with:

Week of AUGUST 29

anger	hope	resignation	self-pity
gratitude	sadness	optimism	other _____

However, at one point in history, there was a band of believers who trusted in someone to change all that. Here was the miracle worker who could command nature, heal sickness, and produce food with a word or a gesture. Here was the King they had believed would reestablish their kingdom. Here on a cross. Dying. And dying with Him were all the hopes they had placed in Him.

From the disciples' perspective, Christ's death gave them no cause to be grateful; there was no call for courage and no reason for optimism. Unless . . . unless, of course, they truly believed Christ for who He said He was and what He said He would do, regardless of the dark circumstances.

Just a few days before Christ's crucifixion He told His followers of His impending death and how He would rise again: "Truly, you will weep and mourn over what is going to happen to me, but the world will rejoice. You will grieve, but your grief will suddenly turn to wonderful joy when you see me again. . . . I have told you all this so that you may have peace in me. Here on earth you will have many trials and sorrows. But take heart, because I have overcome the world" (John 16:20,33).

How has Christ overcome the world? As Son of the sovereign God, He broke the power of death and rose from the dead! God was not caught off guard on that frightful day on Calvary. He knew exactly what He was doing, and He was masterfully in control.

Read in the margin what Jesus told His disciples right before His arrest. Underline the reason they could remain untroubled by the events that were about to take place.

"Don't be troubled. You trust God, now trust in me" (John 14:1).

On a scale of 1 to 10, with 1 being not at all, how easy is it for you to follow Jesus' prescription for remaining untroubled? _____

Jesus knew He was about to die, but He also knew death would have no power over Him. What would seem like a disaster was really for your good because it is through Jesus' atoning death that He will blot out your sins and cancel *your* death notice.

God took an apparent disastrous Friday and turned it into Good Friday—because death had no power over the righteous Son of the sovereign God. Jesus broke the power of death by rising from the grave on the third day, and in doing so pierced the kingdom of darkness with a penetrating light. "And now [God] has made all of this plain to us by the coming of Christ Jesus, our Savior, who broke the power of death and showed us the way to everlasting life" (2 Timothy 1:10).

Christ's resurrection victory over death and despair not only broke the power of death for all of us who trust in Christ as Savior but also provided the means—when we believe in the resurrected Christ as sovereign—for us to receive a whole new perspective of life.

Read 2 Timothy 1:8-12. How does this passage demonstrate Paul had received a new perspective of:

Gratitude? _____

Courage? _____

Optimism? _____

> "We are destined to have our struggles, suffering, and death transformed into blessings, joy, and eternal life."
> —Josh McDowell

You and I and our young people then have the answer to where we are going in life, and in death. For we—every one of us—are *destined to have our struggles, suffering, and death transformed into blessings, joy, and eternal life.*

As we believe with conviction that Christ as sovereign Lord rose from the dead, our perspective on life and death can change, and we can be more than conquerors. Instead of becoming angry, resentful, or losing heart, we can live our lives in the awareness of our destiny, knowing that one day all will be put right. But in order to gain that sense of destiny (and its accompanying spirit of gratitude, courage, and optimism), our kids need to be convinced of the reality of Jesus Christ's resurrection.

**Read Romans 8:35-39.
List the unavoidable tough realities of life found in this passage.** _____

_____

What perspective empowers believers to handle these tough realities? _____

Week of AUGUST 29

The Case of the Empty Tomb: The Stolen-Body Theory

You and I—and our kids—may believe that we are destined to have our struggles, sufferings, and death transformed into blessings, joy, and eternal life. But our destiny can become a reality only if the resurrection of Christ literally took place. In fact, Paul said that "if Christ was not raised, then all our preaching is useless, and your trust in God is useless" (1 Corinthians 15:14). Why? Because if Christ didn't actually rise from the dead, it would be a strong indication that the sacrifice for sin was unacceptable to God and that Christ had not broken the power of death. For if Jesus didn't break the power of death over His own body, how could He cancel our death sentence?

All the great and precious promises are nothing but a fantasy unless Christ truly rose from the dead. Christ's resurrection is a historic necessity if our destiny means anything at all. That is why believing with conviction that Christ literally rose from the dead means knowing that it is actually, factually true. That is what our kids must be convinced of—that is something of which all of us must be convinced.

The evidence of an empty tomb following the crucifixion and burial of Jesus Christ does not by itself prove that Jesus rose from the dead. Yet it does require explanation. Several theories have been offered to explain the empty tomb by those who do not believe Jesus rose from the dead.

> **Read Matthew 28:11-15 and complete the following:**
> 1. **What was one explanation offered within hours of the empty tomb's discovery?** _____
> 2. **Who came up with that explanation?** _____
> 3. **Why do you think they started that rumor?** _____
> _____

The possibility that the disciples stole Jesus' body may seem plausible at first glance. However, the most cursory consideration will quickly show that the stolen-body theory creates more problems than it solves. For example:

- If the guards were sleeping, how could they know whether the disciples—or anyone—stole the body? Sleeping sentinels can't reliably report what happened while they slept.
- Roman soldiers were executed for sleeping on guard duty (which explains Matthew's report of the religious leaders telling the guards, "If the governor hears about it, we'll stand up for you and everything will be all right"). How plausible is it that all the guards at the tomb would have decided to take a nap, knowing it could cost them their lives?
- Even if the Roman guards had slept, consider what it would have taken for thieves to remove Jesus' body from the tomb. The circular stone used to seal the tomb would have weighed between one and two tons! Thieves would have had to sneak past the guards, roll the large stone up a grooved incline, enter the dark tomb, and exit with the body . . . all without waking a single member of the detachment!
- One of the first witnesses on the scene of the empty tomb reported that Jesus' gravecloth was neatly folded and arranged on the burial slab (see John 20:5-8). Can you imagine grave robbers taking the time to meticulously unwrap the body and neatly arrange the cloth on the stone slab? On the contrary, if the body had been stolen, the burial wrappings would certainly have been removed with the body.
- According to the historical accounts, the disciples were incredulous when they heard the news of the empty tomb. From all indications, they were not expecting an empty tomb, much less plotting one.
- Why would a group of men who had run and hidden when their teacher was alive suddenly decide to courageously steal their teacher's body and begin propagating a story that would bring on them the very treatment (arrest, beatings, death) they had fled just three days earlier?

Clearly, the notion that the disciples could or would have stolen Jesus' body while the Roman guards slept strains the bounds of believability.

But if the disciples did not steal Jesus' body, where did it go? If Jesus' body hadn't been resurrected and the religious and political leaders of the day had stolen His body, they could have quickly and effectively quashed the rising sect of Christians by wheeling Christ's corpse through the streets of Jerusalem. This would have been incontrovertible evidence that would have destroyed Christianity practically before it started. But that never happened, which further bolsters the case for the empty tomb, for the enemies of Jesus had every reason to produce His body if they had it.

Week of AUGUST 29

The Case of the Empty Tomb: The Swoon Theory

Some people have tried to explain the empty tomb by suggesting that Jesus never really died. The swoon theory, as it's come to be called, supposes that Jesus was indeed nailed to the cross and suffered tremendous pain and loss of blood. But when He was removed from the cross, He wasn't quite dead; He was merely in shock.

Proponents of this view surmise that the disciples—aided by Joseph of Arimathea—took down the still-living Jesus from the cross and laid Him in the tomb. Then—so the theory goes—Jesus, aided by the cool air of the tomb, by the reviving effects of the burial spices He was wrapped in, and by a day-and-a-half of rest, rose from His own burial slab, cast off His shroud, and left the tomb. When He met His disciples, they mistakenly thought He had risen from the dead (when, in fact, it was nothing more than a surprising resuscitation).

But the swoon theory has several fatal flaws.

THE "DEATH CERTIFICATE"

Jesus had undergone a vicious beating. It was typical for Romans to use an instrument known as a *flagrum,* which often ripped the victim to shreds (many prisoners died before they could be executed, as a result of this scourging). Jesus was then nailed by His hands and feet to a cross.

> **Read Deuteronomy 21:22-23 and John 19:31 in the margin and complete the following:**
>
> **1. The Jewish leaders wanted to hasten the death of the men on the crosses that day because** _____
> _____
>
> **2. Underline what the leaders wanted Pilate to do.**

"If a man guilty of a capital offense is put to death and his body is hung on a tree, you must not leave his body on the tree overnight. Be sure to bury him that same day, because anyone who is hung on a tree is under God's curse" (Deut. 21:22-23, NIV).

"Now it was the day of Preparation, and the next day was to be a special Sabbath. Because the Jews did not want the bodies left on the crosses during the Sabbath, they asked Pilate to have the legs broken and the bodies taken down" (John 19:31).

Then, because the next day was the beginning of the Jewish Passover and Jewish law did not allow them to leave a victim hanging on the cross overnight, the religious leaders asked Pilate to hasten death by ordering that the prisoners' legs be broken (see Deuteronomy 21:22-23; John 19:31). This action usually resulted in death by asphyxiation, as the victim, unable to push up on his feet to relieve the constriction caused by the weight of his body on his lungs, slowly suffocated.

When the crucifixion detail came to break the legs of Jesus, however, they discovered that He was already dead. Nonetheless, to be sure, "one of the soldiers . . . pierced his side with a spear, and blood and water flowed out" (John 19:34). Soon thereafter, when Joseph of Arimathea requested custody of the body, the Roman governor expressed surprise that Jesus was already dead and demanded confirmation. *Only after receiving a firsthand report* did Pilate release the body into the hands of Joseph, thus fully verifying the fact that Jesus was dead before He was buried.

THE GRAVECLOTHS

Jesus' followers prepared His body according to Jewish burial customs. Nicodemus provided "about seventy-five pounds of embalming ointment made from myrrh and aloes. Together [Nicodemus and Joseph] wrapped Jesus' body in a long linen cloth with the spices" (John 19:39-40).

The custom was to wrap the body tightly from the armpits to the ankles, layering the spices—often of a sticky, grimy consistency—between the wrappings. The spices served to preserve the body and acted as an adhesive for the gravecloths. The head was wrapped in a turban-style cloth.

Yet the historical records report that when the empty tomb was discovered on Sunday morning, the first witnesses on the scene saw "the linen wrappings lying there, while the cloth that had covered Jesus' head was folded up and lying to the side" (John 20:6-7).

Accepting the swoon theory would require us to believe that Jesus, having suffered the unspeakable torture of crucifixion, awoke in a dark tomb, maneuvered Himself out of the tightly wound cloths and spices, folded the cloth, laid it on the burial slab, and exited the tomb . . . naked.

THE STONE

Further, Jesus was buried in a rock tomb whose entrance was blocked by a stone weighing perhaps as much as one to two tons.

Week of AUGUST 29

Let's assume Jesus had been taken from the cross in a "swoon," and the cold, damp tomb revived Him sometime later. Let's also assume that He managed to extricate Himself from the unyielding encasement of His burial clothes. We must next assume that once free of those constraints, He managed—from the inside of a tomb designed to be opened only from the outside—to roll a two-ton circular stone up the slotted incline (a difficult job for several men, I would imagine), while somehow propping the stone to prevent it from rolling down again and closing the tomb. All this had to be done by a man who hours before had been flogged, pierced with a crown of thorns, hanged on a cross by nails through His hands and feet, and stabbed in the ribs with a Roman spear. And it had to be done so quietly as to escape the notice of the soldiers who were guarding the tomb, allowing Him to slip away unnoticed.

THE APPEARANCES

On the same day on which Jesus supposedly resuscitated in a cold, damp, dark tomb, unwrapped Himself from the gravecloths, rolled a two-ton stone uphill, and snuck by Roman sentinels guarding the tomb, He also walked more than seven miles from Jerusalem to Emmaus.

Luke 24 records Jesus' appearance to two of His followers who were on the road to Emmaus, a seven-mile trek from Jerusalem. They didn't recognize Jesus until they reached their destination and invited Him to eat with them. When Jesus broke the bread in His customary way, "their eyes were opened, and they recognized him" (Luke 24:31). Walking seven miles to Emmaus is hardly the kind of activity you would expect from a man who had been removed from an executioner's cross and laid in a tomb for more than thirty-six hours.

Yet the appearance of Jesus on the road to Emmaus is only the first in a string of appearances (within days of His brutal experience on the cross) that convinced Jesus' followers that He had defeated death and risen from the dead. As skeptic David Friedrich Strauss—himself no believer in the Resurrection—said, "It is impossible that a being who had stolen half-dead out of the sepulcher, who crept about weak and ill, wanting medical treatment . . . could have given to the disciples the impression that he was a Conqueror over death and the grave, the Prince of Life, an impression which lay at the bottom of their future ministry."[1]

If you desire to dig deeper . . .

Read the following Scriptures. Note to whom Jesus appeared and what He said or did during those appearances.

- Luke 24:13-35
- Luke 24:36-43
- John 20:10-18
- John 20:19-22
- John 20:24-28
- John 21:1-14

THE ASCENSION

If Jesus revived from a deathlike swoon, there is no reason to believe that He later ascended into heaven, as Mark and Luke record. But if Christ didn't ascend, where did He go? Is it reasonable to believe that Jesus withdrew from His followers, to live out the rest of His life in seclusion and die in obscurity?

Such a theory would necessitate the belief that while the young church was preaching the news of Christ's resurrection, Jesus Himself lived in some solitary retreat, unknown to even His closest followers, while His absence perpetuated the legend of Christianity. This scenario would make Jesus Christ—whose teachings extolled the highest standards of morality—the greatest deceiver of all time and His resurrection the greatest hoax in history.

Such a theory also would require believing that Jesus knowingly pursued an insane course of action—contriving His own "resurrection" to gain a renown He would never witness or enjoy.

"After the Lord Jesus had spoken to them, he was taken up into heaven and he sat at the right hand of God" (Mark 16:19).

"When he had led them out to the vicinity of Bethany, he lifted up his hands and blessed them. While he was blessing them, he left them and was taken up into heaven" (Luke 24:50-51).

The Case of the Empty Tomb: The Hallucination Theory

There are only so many ways to explain the empty tomb. If the body wasn't stolen and hidden away and if Jesus didn't swoon and then resuscitate, what else could possibly have happened? Another explanation that has been offered is the hallucination theory.

This theory suggests that those who "saw" Jesus Christ after His death and burial were actually hallucinating. They may have *thought* they saw Jesus alive, but such appearances were the results of hallucination or the power of suggestion.

Hallucinations do occur. People are often mistaken, even deluded, about the things they see or experience. However, there are certain patterns to the experience of delusions and hallucinations. They are highly individualized and extremely subjective. It is exceedingly rare for two persons to experience hallucinations simultaneously.

Week of AUGUST 29

But the accounts of Jesus' resurrection appearances do not bear the marks of a hallucination. The appearances occurred at disparate times. The witnesses were not expecting an appearance and were often puzzled or skeptical at first (see Luke 24:16; John 20:14; John 20:24-25). Jesus appeared at least ten different times following His resurrection. Most of these appearances were to groups of people (see Mark 16:14-18; John 21:1-24; 1 Corinthians 15:6).

Another factor that argues against the hallucination theory is the record of Jesus' invitations to verify His physical presence with them.

Read Luke 24:39-43 in the margin. What proofs served to verify Jesus' physical presence with the disciples? _____

The hallucination theory—like the swoon theory and the stolen-body theory—doesn't stack up against the historical record. Like the other attempts at explanation, it seems to require more faith than it does to believe the testimony of the eyewitnesses: that "during the forty days after his crucifixion, [Jesus] appeared to the apostles from time to time and proved to them in many ways that he was actually alive" (Acts 1:3).

Why do you think it takes more faith to believe the theories discounting Jesus' resurrection than to believe Jesus actually rose from the dead?

_____

> "Look at my hands. Look at my feet. You can see that it's really me. Touch me and make sure that I am not a ghost, because ghosts don't have bodies, as you see that I do! . . . Then he asked them, 'Do you have anything here to eat?' They gave him a piece of broiled fish, and he ate it as they watched" (Luke 24:39-43).

What Does It All Mean?

Remember the most fundamental questions of life: Who am I? Why am I here? and Where am I going? What God is saying to each of us through His incarnation, reliable Word, and the bodily resurrection of His Son answers these questions. What does this mean for you and me and our young people who believe in Christ and His Word with conviction?

1. God Wants a Relationship with Us.

Separated from God, we were all adrift, without a sense of connection, not knowing who we really were. Yet Christ entered our world as the Incarnate One and revealed to us our true identity, an identity that had been lost due to sin and death. He adopted us back into His family, so that each of us can have a personal relationship with Him and truly say, "I know who I am: God's chosen child who loves Him and others as only I can."

2. God Wants Us to Know Him and Be Like Him.

God's Holy Spirit inhabits our lives, and as a personal "truth guide" He is leading us through the relational revelation of God's reliable Word so we can know God better as His divine power transforms us more and more into the family image of His Son. We are to no longer live self-serving lives with actions that disgrace ourselves and our families but are to live lives that are pleasing to God. No longer aimless and without a clear purpose, we have gained that sense of completeness so each of us can say, "I know why I'm here: to know God and become more like Him."

3. God Wants Us to Trust Him, No Matter What.

Because He lives, we can face tomorrow—not with uncertainty, anger, or pessimism, but with a sense of destiny, confident that our risen Savior and sovereign God causes all things to work together for our good and His glory. Without a doubt each of us can say, "I know where I'm going: destined to have my struggles, sufferings, and death transformed into blessings, joys, and eternal life."

This kind of faith with deepened convictions in Christ and His Word results in a personal identity, sense of purpose, and eternal perspective that can help us face whatever comes our way, knowing that we are children of a King, being readied to inherit a kingdom not of this world.

If you have enjoyed these studies from Josh McDowell and desire to purchase your own copy of his book Beyond Belief to Convictions to read and study in greater detail, visit the LifeWay Christian Store serving you. Or, you can order a copy by calling 1-800-233-1123.

Summarize how each biblical truth relates to the fundamental question of life:

The Incarnation to Who am I? _____

God's reliable Word to Why am I here? _____

The bodily resurrection of God's Son to Where am I going? _____

[1] David Friedrich Strauss, *The Life of Jesus for People*, 2d ed., vol. 1 (London: William & Norgate, 1879), 412.

Week of AUGUST 29

NOTES

To the Leader:

Pray for each participant in your class by name. Write notes to or e-mail persons you pray for, assuring them of your prayers for them this week. Invite them to share specific requests with you if they desire.
Also encourage them to come to the new study that begins next Sunday.

Before the Session

1. Read "During the Session." Choose the teaching steps you will use.
2. Adequately acquaint yourself with the three false theories concerning the Resurrection introduced on Days 2,3,4. Be aware of the arguments for each theory and its weaknesses.

During the Session

1. Welcome participants. Open with prayer requests and prayer.
2. Encourage adults to share their pet peeves. Ask, *Why do these petty annoyances cause us to lose our perspective?* Allow discussion. Then as learners, *What are major issues that make it easy to lose perspective?* Allow discussion. Then ask, *What are some possible responses to life's difficulties and tragedies?* Write responses on the board. Ask, *What did Dr. McDowell say are desirable responses to the tough realities of life?* Write responses on the board, being certain to include Gratitude, Courage, and Optimism.
3. Ask, *Whose perspective must we have to be grateful, courageous, and optimistic in trying times?* Invite someone to read Isaiah 55:8-9. Ask, *How can we view life from God's perspective if He sees things so differently from us?* After a brief discussion of that question, read Isaiah 55:10-13 and instruct the class to listen for what God desires for our lives. [Joy and peace] Request someone read Romans 8:35-39 and allow volunteers to share their responses to the last activity of Day 1. Discuss how the godly perspectives of unconditional love, joy, and peace will enable believers to handle this life with gratitude, courage, and optimism.
4. Ask someone to read the quotation in the margin of Day 1 on page 158. Ask, *What must we believe in with absolute conviction if our destiny is to become a reality?* [Christ's Resurrection]
5. Organize the class into three groups. Ask Group One to use Scripture and logic presented in this week's lesson to refute the Stolen-Body Theory (Day 2). Ask Group Two to do the same with The Swoon Theory (Day 3). Ask Group Three to refute the

NOTES

Hallucination Theory (Day 4). Allow several moments for groups to work and then request the groups share with the whole class what each theory suggests, why it is insufficient to explain the Resurrection, and what they discussed. [Be prepared to supplement the explanations of each theory and the theory's weaknesses.]

6. Optional step: Prepare a mini-lecture on each of the three false theories about the Resurrection (Days 2,3,4). Be sure to explain each view and tell why it is inadequate. Consider listing the weaknesses of each theory on the board. [Note: Whether small groups report or you offer a mini-lecture, make sure learners are acquainted with the Jewish burial customs explained on pages 162-163.]

7. State that the only logical conclusion is that the resurrection of Jesus actually occurred. Discuss: *How does the Resurrection give you cause for gratitude? How does it empower you to be courageous? What reasons does it give you to be optimistic when life is so hard? How does the Resurrection enable you to see life from God's perspective?*

8. Ask learners to name all of Jesus' post-resurrection appearances they can remember. List these on the board. Say, *Jesus appeared at least ten different times following His resurrection.* Use the "If you desire to dig deeper" exercise under Day 3 (page 163) to see who were some of the persons Jesus appeared to and what He said or did in those appearances.

9. Ask learners to review the content of Day 5. Inquire: *As a result of our study of* Beyond Belief to Conviction *what insight have you gained into your true identity? your purpose? your destiny? How do you feel better equipped to reach today's young people for Christ as a result of this study?* Allow time for discussion.

10. Close in prayer, thanking God for His salvation. Ask for the courage and optimism to face life from His perspective and to share the good news that a relationship with God is real, relevant, and right now.

After the Session

1. Read next week's lesson and complete the learning activities.
2. Recruit several active members to help you contact absentees and prospects this week. Take each person a copy of next quarter's *MasterWork* and promote the exciting new studies by Charles Stanley, T. W. Hunt, and Claude King that begin next week.

Further in-depth Bible studies by the authors presented this quarter in masterWork are available in their full-length books.

The God Who Loves
JOHN MacARTHUR, JR.

Beyond Belief to Convictions
JOSH MCDOWELL & BOB HOSTETLER

To purchase your own copies to read and study, visit the LifeWay Christian Store serving you. Or, you can order these books by calling 1-800-233-1123.

master\Work

ESSENTIAL MESSAGES FROM GOD'S SERVANTS

Ever notice how God works in the lives of various believers? Realizing that God is at work in the world, some of God's servants determine to join Him in sharing deeper spiritual insights into God's message as it works in and through their lives.

master\Work seeks to identify key biblically based messages that have come out of the heart of God's servants. You and your friends can now study and experience these messages. Every quarter in master\Work, life messages of essential value for believers will be provided to help you live a vital and growing Christian life.

Your church can use master\Work to support the Lord's work of knowing God, transforming believers, and growing your Sunday School or small group ministry.

Invite your friends to join you in learning how to bring purpose to life through a meaningful relationship with Jesus Christ.

If you desire other approaches to Bible study, learn about other LifeWay resources, such as our *Explore the Bible* series, *Family Bible Study* series, and *Life Connections* series (Bible studies that build community) on www.lifeway.com.

COMING NEXT QUARTER

Don't miss the exciting Bible study lessons next quarter drawn from Charles Stanley's *How to Handle Adversity* and T. W. Hunt and Claude King's *In God's Presence*.

ISBN 0-6330-9089-1

9 780633 090890